John Janaway will be a familiar figure to anyone with even a passing interest in the local and family history of Surrey, where he has lived all his life. For seventeen years he was the Surrey Local Studies Librarian, based at Guildford, and his work took him all over the county and beyond, meeting fellow local historians, and presenting his colourful and much acclaimed talks to societies, groups and gatherings. He is the author of a number of popular books, including *Surrey Murders, Ghosts of Surrey, Surrey – A County History* and *Surrey Privies*. In 1998 he took early retirement in order to concentrate on his writing and on the running of a very successful small publishing company.

SURREY
BEDSIDE BOOK

*A Collection of Prose
and Poetry*

SELECTED AND INTRODUCED BY
JOHN JANAWAY

THE DOVECOTE PRESS

First published in 2002 by The Dovecote Press Ltd
Stanbridge, Wimborne, Dorset BH21 4JD

ISBN 1 904349 07 2

Typeset in Monotype Sabon
Printed and bound in Singapore

A CIP catalogue record for this book is available
from the British Library

1 3 5 7 9·8 6 4 2

CONTENTS

INTRODUCTION

I suppose that the ideal book for reading at bedtime must contain a varied collection of material just sufficient to fascinate the mind without over-stimulating the brain, and it must relieve the memory of the irritations and over-demands of the day just ending. It should be something you can read from the middle to the end and back again or the other way round without losing the plot. It must cater for those who like to sample here and there, but it must also be structured for those who do insist on reading it from front to back. The pieces must be reasonably short (or very short for when you're really tired) but leave the mind with positive thoughts as you switch out the light. If you are like me, a good novel cannot be put down and the bedside light stays firmly on until three in the morning. That is not what this book is about.

This book is a very personal selection which makes no claim to contain all that is acknowledged as the best in poetry and prose relating to the county of Surrey. Yes, it contains some well-known extracts, which I have found difficult to leave out, but I have also tried to search out new items to give a different insight into this unique county of ours. Here I hope that you will find intriguing information as well as relaxation, food for thought and perhaps the occasional smile.

Although it might have been tempting to select my pieces solely from a readily available array of books, I have also made use of material not always associated with bedtime reading. For example, here you will find snippets extracted from a range of newspapers and cuttings dating from the early eighteenth to the twentieth centuries. Over the years I have ferreted them away in the hope that they would, one day, be useful and now, perhaps, they are.

It seems that Parliament has frequently delighted in re-arranging the map of Surrey. Many people, including those who live in the county or think they do, are often confused about what is and what is not

Surrey. For my area I have taken the present administrative county but not that part across the Thames which, until 1965, was firmly in the ancient but now sadly defunct county of Middlesex. I apologise to all of you from Staines, Ashford, Sunbury and Shepperton but you deserve a bedside book of your own! To the present county area I have added those places which remained in Surrey after the formation of London County Council in 1889 but were lost to our county in 1965, when the ill-fated Greater London Council was established. These include Kingston upon Thames, Richmond and Croydon.

As usual, nothing in print is arrived at without the readily proffered help of friends and former colleagues. Many thanks are therefore due to the staff of the Surrey History Centre at Woking, to Surrey Archaeological Society and their assistant librarian, Sheila Ashcroft, to Brian Boyd, Jeff Harwood, Maureen Roberts and, of course, to my wife, Sue.

Finally, I hope that you enjoy this book enough to stay awake until you turn out the light.

JOHN JANAWAY, *October* 2002

I · LANDSCAPE AND CHARACTER

Surrey from the Historian

John Aubrey's The Natural History and Antiquities of Surrey *was the first comprehensive history of Surrey. It was published posthumously in five volumes in 1718-19, although Aubrey began compiling the work in about 1673. In Aubrey's time, of course, the county of Surrey stretched north to the Thames at Southwark, at the southern end of London Bridge. The area of the county has shrunk considerably since then and large tracts of land have been lost to London in two stages. Firstly, in 1889, when London County Council came into being and, secondly, in 1965, with the creation of the ill-fated Greater London Council. However, a portion of the defunct county of Middlesex was added to Surrey in 1965. Finally, a bite was taken out of Surrey's southern boundary when Gatwick Airport was transferred to West Sussex in 1974.*

This County is called *Surrey*, i.e. *Suthrey* in *Saxon*, from its Situation on the South Side of the *River:* It was under the *Romans*, with *Sussex*, stiled *Regni*, as some say, because their generous Conquerors granted them their former Priviledge of living under a *Regal* or *Kingly* Government: It is called by Venerable *Bede* Suthriona; and is bordered on the East by *Kent*, on the West by the Counties of *Berks* and

Southampton, on the South by *Sussex*, and Northward by *Middlesex*, from which it is separated by the River *Thames*. This County is the most Part very fruitful and pleasant, as to that part situate on the *Thames*; neither can it be stiled barren in the open Champain in Corn or Hay. In it you have a very agreeable Variety of Woods, Fields, Hills, and Meadows, interspersed throughout the whole Limits: It has been likened by some to a coarse Cloth with a rich Bordure or Fringe, the inner Part being less fruitful than the Skirts . . .

The Middle of the County is in Latitude of 51 degr. 15 min. and the Longitude from *London* 20 min. It contains thirteen Hundreds, eight Market Towns, 140 Parishes, 35 Vicarages, 449 Villages and Hamlets; is watered by the Rivers of *Thames*, *Mole*, and *Wey*, and produces in Plenty *Wallnuts*, *Fullers Earth*, *Box*, and *Corn*, and contains 592000 Acres of Land. The several Towns are, under the King, governed by their Magistrates, Lords of the Manour, &c. but the whole is under the Direction of a Lord Lieutenant, *Custos Rotulorum*, and a High Sheriff . . .

John Aubrey, The Natural History and Antiquities of Surrey.

Surrey from the Architect

Surrey is one of those English counties that will not fit into the traditional pattern. It was so remote in the Middle Ages that it does not possess a large medieval parish church; yet today there is hardly anywhere in the county where one can feel free of London. It has been in the forefront of English architecture only once, in 1900, and has since seen the endless debased multiplication of the type of building it pioneered. A history of English medieval architecture could be written without once mentioning a surviving Surrey building; a history of the suburb or the folly could almost be written without going outside the county. All through the county there are these paradoxes and somehow Surrey always seems to get the worst of the bargain.

This may be too gloomy a picture, for there is plenty of architecture to see in Surrey, but it is very often the small, the picturesque, or the *recherché*. And Surrey landscape is exactly those things. . . there is a remarkable variety in both scenery and geology. What is spoilt is utterly spoilt, what is left alone, or more often vigorously preserved, is enchanting. Certainly in one respect – for varied short-distance walks – it is difficult to match Surrey anywhere. Five miles will often take in as many different types of landscape. All the ridges in Surrey run from W to E, and hence the landscape, though intricate, is never tortuous and involved in the way that West Dorset is. The pattern is followed quite regularly through the county, though it sometimes takes a sharp eye to spot the transitions.

Ian Nairn and Nikolaus Pevsner, The Buildings of England: Surrey, *2nd edition (1971).*

A Rural Ride from Chertsey to Merrow in 1822

William Cobbett is best known for his Rural Rides, *first published in 1830, but he was also a prolific political commentator and wrote on a diverse range of subjects. He was born at Farnham in 1762 and died at Normandy, near Guildford, in 1835.*

At Chertey, where we came into Surrey again, there was a Fair for horses, cattle, and pigs. I did not see any sheep. Everything was exceedingly *dull*. Cart colts, two and three years old, were selling for *less than a third* of what they sold for in 1813. The cattle were of an inferior description to be sure; but the price was low almost beyond belief. Cows, which would have sold for 15*l*. in 1813, did not get buyers at 3*l*. I had no time to inquire much about the pigs, but a man told me that they were dirt-cheap . . .

This county of Surrey presents to the eye of the traveller a greater contrast than any other county in England. It has some of the very best and some of the very worst lands, not only in England, but in the world. We were here upon those of the latter description. For five miles on the road towards Guildford the land is a rascally common covered with poor heath, except where the gravel is so near the top as not to suffer even the heath to grow. Here we entered the enclosed lands, which have the gravel at bottom, but a nice light, black mould at top; in which the trees grow very well. Through bye-lanes and bridle-ways we came out into the London road, between Ripley and Guildford, and immediately crossing that road, came on towards a village called Merrow.

William Cobbett, Rural Rides *(1830).*

The Surrey Shepherd near the British Camp (1901)

Suburban London has stretched out its fingers so far into the lovely county of Surrey that one now hardly expects to be able to study genuine shepherd life within twenty miles of Charing Cross. Yet such was my good fortune one cold spring morning in the year 1901. I had cycled out as far as the escarpment of the North Downs, to search for vestiges of an ancient British camp. The weather and the scenery were alike grand. After the first dozen miles had been traversed, I took a by-road which led through a delightful downland valley, shut in by smooth billowy ridges and domes of chalk. A stiff climb now began, and the road gradually ascended until, at a height of about 600 feet, I reached the famous Pilgrims' Way, the Mediæval road to Canterbury from the West. Thereabout is a small upland village, and back in the fields is the plain barn-like church, devoid of a steeple, but quietly attractive because of its probable associations with the pilgrims. These unpretentious churches are often overlooked by tourists – they are so remote and so retiring and seem to promise little of interest.

The region, since that date partly given over to modern mansions, was then sparsely inhabited – the total population of the village was only about six score – and though of great charm to those who take with them pleasures half-made, would be rather dreary to folk of ordinary tastes. Passing forward a mile or two, the country became even less populous, and as the Ordnance map indicated that the goal was not far distant, I asked an aged hedger the way to War Coppice. He was just finishing some slight meal, perhaps that which the Essex labourer calls 'elevens', and was resting awhile. He wore a stout pair of leather leggings which fitted tightly. His gloves and trimming knife lay on the bank under the projecting roots of a beech tree. He did not answer at once, but began to fill his blackened pipe, slowly, not only because of the burden of years, but because his hands were gnarled and knotty, and his poor bent fingers were no longer fitted for light operations. At last he replied, but his instructions were rambling and I could plainly see that they would soon take me in a direction exactly opposite to the one desired. 'You won't get that way', said he, in answer to a hesitating objection on my part, 'it's all like this', that is, all like the flinty rubble in the roadside gutter. He had 'heard' of a 'battle' which was fought somewhere near, but the simple fact was that he did not know the prehistoric spot by the name printed on the map, and, like many others of his kind, would not freely confess his ignorance. 'No, no, you must go this way', was his final decision.

Perverse, because I had faith in the map, I went onward for another quarter of an hour, until, on the very brow of the hill, through the ground mist there came the tinkle of a bell, and a flock of sheep slowly straggled across the road. The upper portion of a human shape then appeared in the murk and

'Wilder'd o'er the waste

The shepherd stalked, gigantic.'

Seen at close quarters the giant proved to be a short, cheery apple-faced man of seventy or seventy-five. He carried a crook, Sussex fashion, and was accompanied by a black collie. Considering it prudent to vary my question, I asked, 'Where does this road lead, please?' 'Most anywhere,' was the comprehensive reply. This way leads to Caterham, to the right is a well-known private park, round the flank of the hill is such a farm, a lime-pit lies below, and the Pilgrims' Way is 'back there', but the earthwork is not known. At once I fixed him to the 'Pilgrims' Way', because it has been denied that peasants do not spontaneously employ the term that, in fact, it has been foisted upon them from outside. Here, apparently, was a genuine case of folk-memory, for he knew the lie of the road, and the spot where it had been ploughed up thirty years before, nay, he asserted that he could take you all along the track from Merstham to Knockholt.

I asked him about War Coppice. 'No, I never 'eard of that, but I know where the battle was fought, by the side of that there wood.' Ah, then, the encampment which I sought must be somewhere near. 'Yes, it's bound to be, but the battle was a long while ago, and they fought in that wood. Leastways, they allus says a battle was fought there, but it was afore my time, by a long way.' No wonder that he does not know 'War Coppice', for he does not 'belong to this part'.

'Then you were not born in Surrey?' 'I was born at Chaldon' – a village only a few miles away. Then, seeing my look of surprise, he continued, in a tone of deprecation, 'But I only came here two years ago'. In two years one could not be expected to know in detail the topography of a district four miles from one's birthplace! His next statement was amazing: he had never been ten miles from the spot where he now stood since he was as many years old. Before that time, while still a small boy, he had 'once or twice been with the team to London', but that was a London, one calls to mind, which was only just beginning to get accustomed to railways, and which was still largely served by waggons, market carts, and barges. There was one notable exception – the iron tramroad, first of its kind, from Merstham to Wandsworth, in which horse-drawn vehicles were used to expedite the transport of such goods as lime, corn and coal . . .

He had lately been busy among the lambs, and had had some terribly severe weather. It would almost seem that the old tale of the wind bringing the lambs had come true. Only short snatches of sleep could he steal when he took shelter in his trundle hut. Two, three, four times a night had he been compelled to go round the straw-hurdled compound to attend newly-born lambs, to succour the ewes, to prepare cosy bedding on the lee side of the innermost pens. But he had been fairly lucky; there was a good proportion of pairs, and his master was quite satisfied.

Even now there was a shrewd nip in the morning air, and as I looked at the weather-beaten, yet not discontented, face of the shepherd, I called to mind the reproachful eloquence which Jacob poured out against his oppressor, and the words haunted me for some time afterwards. 'Thus I was; in the day the drought consumed me, and the frost by night; and my sleep departed from mine eyes.' Whoever has been forced to keep awake night after night, or has even had his slumbers repeatedly broken, can appreciate the poignancy of these words, and their close application to the shepherd's life in the late days of winter.

Speaking for myself, the man's words went home, for earlier in the year, at a spot not far away, I had examined the arrangements made for the shepherd and his flock during the lambing season. Below a beech plantation on yonder hill, the farmer, looking well ahead last autumn, had left a large rick of barley, which, when threshed, yielded a fine stack of straw. This stack, for several reasons, was then purposely enclosed within the large lambing pen, or to be strictly correct, it was made to form part of the boundary fence. On the sheltered side of the rick, and therefore within the fenced space, stood the shepherd's hut, well screened from the northern blasts. There, too, were fixed the special pens for invalid sheep and weakling lambs untimely born. The barley straw provided not only soft litter, but to some extent a choice change of diet for the ewes, for they would be glad to 'pick it over' in the time of frost and blizzards. Hard by the shepherd's hut was a warm recess for orphan yeanlings; these tremulous mites had to be coaxed to drink warm milk, which was usually kept simmering in readiness.

Taking into consideration all the difficulties to be solved, the wheeled hut was a moderately comfortable place on a windy evening. Sacks laid on straw formed a rude couch, if haply the shepherd dare go to sleep. It need not be said that he could never take off his clothes at this season. A candle would be burning, and spare ones were always in readiness. There was a stove for heating his own food, or milk for the lambs. The iron stove pipe was bent at right angles, and passed through the top of the hut to carry away the smoke, so that there was little irritation of eyes and nose, nevertheless the hut might often become unpleasantly hot. On a shelf above the bed were the man's rations for the next twelve hours or more – bread, cheese, meat, beer, or a can of tea to be warmed when wanted. A second shelf served as tool-box and medicine chest, and here one saw shears, hammer and nails, a clasp-knife, raddle or ruddle, a pot of sheep-salve, another of tar, a box of ground ginger, a bottle of turpentine, and another of castor oil. A saucepan was suspended from a hook, and in the corner stood a crowbar . . .

The scarp face of the downs beneath our feet is fluted into a series of rounded scallops, buttressed in such a manner that one might fancy a giant had tooled and smoothed the soft material. Everywhere around these slopes, even up to the crest of the down, are tiny concentric tracks, sweeping along with the curve of the hill, These miniature path-ways, one above the other, have been formed by the sheep, which proverbially follow their leader, and which like to graze on the level, rarely ascending the hill vertically . . .

The loose, straggling hedgerows of hawthorn, dogwood, spindle, climbing rose, clematis, and wayfaring tree, are altogether unpleached, and the banks below them are broken and disintegrated by rabbit tunnels. From the time when the hawthorns were first allowed to spring up, in the early days of enclosures, when, as likely as not, these boundaries linked up the rows of yews and wayfaring trees, the hedgerows have suffered little diminuation, save at the hand of firewood collectors. The shepherd says that he can remember the time when part of this region was open downland, used mainly for sheep runs. The country would then resemble the naked downs around Eastbourne or Lewes. Those readers who are familiar with the writings of Arthur Young and William Marshall can picture the process of enclosure with tolerable accuracy, and indeed, it would only require the felling of a hedgerow here and a coppice there, and the removal of a short wall yonder, to restore the prehistoric wildness of the place. The Napoleonic Wars led to much second-rate land being put under the plough, and it was long before the well-paid farmer would allow the cultivated fields to revert to pasture. Hence, while our friend speaks of the old bare sheep-walks, such as those of Banstead and Woodmansterne, often alluded to by the poets, and referred to in the ditty 'Sutton for good mutton, Cheam for juicy beef', he can likewise point out portions of the down where open arable fields once existed.

The 'Banstead Downs mutton', that 'most relishing dainty' as an old writer called it, was reputed to get its fine flavour from the wild thyme and juniper of the district, but there is little juniper on those downs to-day. Further afield, at Box Hill and Bookham and Newlands Corner and Merrow, the shrub grows in abundance. As a boy, the shepherd went leasing – a fine old Biblical word for gleaning – in fields now overrun by wild grasses, differing in species from, and somewhat coarser than those of the surrounding slopes. Nowadays the farmers, he says, grow little more corn than they require for themselves and their cattle.

Near the spot where he used to go leasing, pheasants are now reared for sport. 'But, law bless ye, I doon't call pheasant-shooting spoort; the birds just lobber up in front of you and you knocks 'em down. That's not spoort.'

The shepherd's talk about the open fields of the mid-nineteenth century quite corroborated what I had heard in other parts of the county, as for instance, in the district of the Bookhams, the Horsleys, Caterham and Woodmansterne. The doggerel rhyme about Sutton and mutton, before quoted, had meaning only when Sutton, Cheam, Carshalton, and Caterham were small villages . . .

The flock has silently stolen away into the dry coombe, whence a gentle tintinnabulation still reaches the ear. The vapour has meanwhile been clearing, but a faint, nebulous cloud of fine dust impregnated with the characteristic and unmistakable odour of wool, has taken its place. The herdsman must needs follow his charges, and after a hearty 'Good day' on each side, I am left alone. Not a single human being is now to be seen. Far away to the South stretches the Weald of Surrey and Sussex, still thinly veiled in a gauzy, diaphanous mantle of mist. The querulous cry of a peewit in a distant ploughed field is barely distinguishable, and, were it not for the gladsome lark, and a little nut brown wren, which has just reeled off a scolding tirade to its mate in the hedge-bank, the silence would be complete.

Walter Johnson, Talks with Shepherds *(1925). There are few sheep on the North Downs today, but flocks are still to be found in some parts of south-west Surrey.*

The Meaning of Agricultural Depression

What is the meaning of agricultural depression? I look upon the year 1879 as a sort of visitation. As to the seasons, they have worked very true since the years 1814 and 1816: in the one there was a great drought, and in the other a great deal of wet, according to what my father told me. And since that we have had the potato famine as a sort of visitation, and the rinderpest, which was a great loss to the farmers.

As to foot and mouth disease, I know the public think the remedy is worse that the disease; for where the stock is properly seen to, there is seldom any fatal cases. As for putting a stop to the markets, that throws a great stagnation on trade throughout the country. What the council can be thinking about I cannot understand! The farmers can't have their stock stocked.

I myself had two cows that wanted to be driven, and I had to go three miles to the policemen, and when I got there he was not at home. The result was I couldn't take them, so lost the chance.

Now, there are hundreds served the same way, and we shall feel the effects for a long time. As for stamping it out, that is very unreasonable. There always were plagues, and will be all the time there is so much dilatoriness in our farmyards and rickyards.

I once heard a valuer say that a good cleared-up rickyard, with the ricks well thatched, was worth a hundred pounds a year to a farmer. But I am sorry to say there is scarcely one to be found anywhere. Since they had the machinery they let their kavins lay in a lump and rot, and their strawricks left open to the weather. Then the stock lie down on the wet straw, and the result is they take cold and get fever on them, and then have the foot and mouth disease.

Then, again, the farmers take more land than they can properly cultivate, and a great deal of it is laying dormant; it produces nothing but yellow moss and thistles. The farmer has to pay the same rent, tithe, and taxes as he does for the land that grows more produce; and I am sorry they lose it in that way – that it does no one any good.

'A Carrier's Boy' [Eli Hamshire], The Source of England's Greatness and the Source of England's Poverty (1892). Arguments over the best way to defeat foot and mouth seem unchanged in over a hundred years.

A Surrey Farmhouse

Arthur Trower was born in a farmhouse called 'Wiggie' near Redhill, returning to live there after the death of his parents.

Well do I remember the Saturday nights of my boyhood. I fancy I am again in the old chimney corner in our typically farm-house kitchen. I suppose I am hardly justified in calling it 'comfortable,' for though it often was very comfortable indeed, yet there were occasions when, as it had four doors which opened north, south, east, and west, there was at times too strong a draught to make it an ideally cosy spot. Nevertheless, on Saturday nights, when the week's work was ended, and the kitchen, spotlessly clean and tidy, had put on its look of homely restfulness, it would not have been lightly passed by, had any lover of the quaint and picturesque by chance or invitation looked in upon us. For my part, I have seen few places that were either more inviting or more difficult to leave. But I am speaking of my boyhood's days and must proceed. From my snug little den in the old chimney corner, I can peer upwards into the black darkness, where in winter the north wind roars and howls, and where I know there is a mysterious chamber in which our bacon is undergoing the process of being smoked. The log on the fire is lazily smouldering away and its white ash only serves to show up more prominently the black polished grate. The steel fire-irons shine like burnished glass, vieing in this respect with the snow white platters on the dresser opposite.

The walls, defaced with no tawdry prints, are bare of ornaments, save for the polished metal dish covers which pleasantly reflect the genial glow of the fireside opposite, the old weather glass, and my father's favourite muzzle-loaders . . .

The old grandfather clock, with his sober tick, seems to exercise quite a soporific influence, and all save he are perfectly still. Seated at the long, low, spotlessly clean table is my father, with his wages book and pile of silver before him, while, busily plying her needle, my mother sits close by.

It is a very simple scene I wish to portray, and yet it speaks to us of quiet happiness and homely peace. One by one the labourers come forward to take their wages, and I seem to hear again the sound of their measured tread, as, in their heavy boots, they come along the lobby and across the scullery floor, bringing with them the scent of the hay-stack, the cowshed, or the grain pit.

Many a year have some of them worked 'fur measter,' and on pay nights there is always a little bit of chat before finally ending up the week.

The weather, the crops, and the stock practically exhaust the subjects of conversation. The weather was always the chief topic, and, strange to say, the signs were always very ominous.

Was rain badly wanted the wind was in the east, and would 'very like' stay there for several weeks. If we were in the middle of splendid harvest weather, they were 'afeared' we shouldn't be long 'afore we had a chainge.'

Of course the moon was generally the malign influence at work, and surely no belief was ever more deeply rooted than this time-honoured fallacy concerning the earth's weather changes and the moon.

'I reckon we'll have a chainge afore very long, Measter,' I remember one old weather-beaten prophet remarking one Saturday evening, long before any change came.

'What makes you think so, Tom?' asked my father. 'I doan't like the leuk o' the moon,' replied he, 'she's a-lyin' a deal too much on her back.'

This old-fashioned belief dies very hard, and I am firmly persuaded that so far as our country villagers are concerned, the moon will continue to dominate our weather long after we have passed away.

St. Swithin, of course, was a red-letter saint with our old labourers. Indeed, no doubt the veracity of that famous old legend was, in their eyes, proof positive, not so much of imbecility, as of pitiable ignorance. I have said that most of them were quite unable to read or write, and hence all their calculations were based on rough and ready methods in which memory played the chief part.

Thus the farming operations were all controlled by the dates of the neighbouring fairs. These fairs, indeed, were most important in the old-time labourer's life, and themselves not without influence on the weather, though their chief use in his calendar was to settle the times of planting or sowing. Thus scarlet runner beans were always planted at Crawley spring fair time, and cabbage seed sown on July 15th, the date of the extinct Bletchingley fair. Like many another old custom the holding of these fairs is fast dying out, and apparently (though I hope not) in our great-grandchildren's time will only exist as tradition.

Arthur Trower, Our Homestead and Its Old World Garden *(1910). It's sad to report that the fairs died out much more quickly than the author prophesied.*

Hop-pickers

On September 2, 1806, I was one of three friends who agreed to visit Farnham in Surrey, for the purpose of seeing the commencement of the hop-picking. It is known that hop-plantations of that place afford the most delicate samples of that article, and of the highest price in the markets; which is attributed, in addition to a favourable soil and situation, to singular care in the gathering and drying, and to pulling them at a period somewhat previous to their full maturity. To the latter cause, particularly, is owing the distinguished flavour and fragrancy of the Farnham hops.

Of our journey down, little needs to be said, for it was by the road through Hounslow and Bagshot, across some of the dreariest heaths in the kingdom. There is much beauty of prospect, however, beyond Staines, on approaching the precincts of Windsor forest. We found the road enlivened for some miles about Egham, by people flocking to the races, held on the celebrated Runnymede, a corner of which we crossed, having in view the race-booths and assembled company. I could not surppress a wish that this spot of ground, consecrated to English freedom by the signature of Magna Charta, had been distinguished by some more appropriate memorial than being made the scene of a common diversion.

From beyond Shrubs-hill to the neighbourhood of Farnham an almost uninterupted chain of black heaths extends, presenting for miles not a trace of cultivation. Over the widest part, the Basingstoke canal passes, which, it may be hoped, will in time convey improvement into these deserts, at present the reproach and deformity of the country. The solitude of the scene was enlivened to us, by the circumstance of overtaking some waggons more fully laden with human beings than we had almost ever beheld. These consisted mostly of the female sex, of all ages, collected from Hampshire, Berkshire, and other districts, and proceeding to the hop-picking at Farnham. It seems, it is the custom for the growers to make musters of people in the villages, who assemble at an appointed place and time, when waggons are sent for their conveyance. The drivers of these living cargoes had their hats decorated with ribbons, and flags were placed in the front of the vehicles, from which, as we passed, we were saluted with a medley of jocund cries and screams.

The approach to Farnham is a striking contrast to the desolate tract preceding it. For a considerable way the road lies between continued ranges of hop-gardens, which were now in their utmost beauty; and certainly, few objects of vegetable culture can vie with the hop in elegance. The dark leaf of the plant finely sets off the pale apple-green of the catkin or hop, the brightness of which was this year generally uninjured by rust or mildew. Nothing could exceed the luxuriance of the loaded sprays, mounting above the tops of the poles, or hanging down in long festoons. The paths between the rows presented long green avenues, seeming to end in an impervious wood, and often crossed at the summit of the poles by meeting sprays.

The town of Farnham is of pretty considerable extent, running along the bottom of a valley, through which the small stream of the Wey takes its winding course, bordered by green meadows. On each side, the ground rises with a steep slope, along which the hop-plantations spread down into the valley, and even into the streets of the town, which may be said to be built in a hop-garden. On the north side, a street leads from the centre up to the castle, or bishop of Winchester's palace, a venerable mansion which crowns the eminence. Contiguous to it are the remains of an ancient fortress, once a place of great strength. From the palace a park extends, occupying the high ground which forms that side of the valley, and presenting a long avenue of lofty trees cresting the summit. The park possesses an agreeable variety of ground laid out with taste, and is stocked with a fine herd of deer.

We had not long arrived, before we witnessed the entrance of one of the transport waggons. The best drest girls were seated in the front, singing in full chorus; and the whole calvalcade had an air of festivity not usual among English peasantry. We soon proceeded to a large plantation above the town, at which the picking was just commenced. On the exterior edge of the ground a numerous band of pickers was ranged, divided into groups, each seated round great baskets, into which the women and children were pulling the hops, as they were brought clinging to the poles by men, who were seen occasionally emerging from the plantation. It was a lively and picturesque scene.

The Athenæum (1807). Hop growing in the Farnham area went into a steep decline in the twentieth century. However, a hop garden survived at nearby Puttenham, on the southern slopes of the Hog's Back, and recently the acreage there has been increased.

Memories of Harvest Time

Gertrude Jekyll, the famous gardener, was also a talented author, embroiderer, artist, and keen observer of country life and the ways of country people. However, she is best remembered for the gardens she created around the houses designed by Edwin Lutyens. She lived at Munstead near Godalming and died in 1932.

The threshing of corn on the barn floor was one of the happiest of country sights and sounds. From after harvest to the spring of the next year, stored in the ample bays of the barn, it could be threshed out as it was wanted, hand-winnowed, and put away in the granary.

The granaries themselves of the older fashion are beautiful buildings. I am thankful that on many farms they are still standing, though buildings so perfectly in harmony with the sentiment of rural English life are now rarely erected. They are usually over a waggon-shed, carried upon short piers with rat-proof caps of stone or oak. Rough stone steps lead up to the granary door and add much to the pictorial value of the building.

Indeed, in these sad days of cheap building, and corrugated iron roofing, and machinery, one looks in vain for many of the lost beauties of country life. Women, gleaning in the harvest-field – 'leasing' as they used to call it – are now no longer seen. The pitiless, grasping iron contrivances pick up the stray ears too closely. The mower carrying his scythe is to be remembered only, for he is rarely to be met.

In the older days the wives and children of farm-servants were allowed to glean or 'lease' on the fields of the farm where the father was employed, before the sheaves were carried. If others came who were not entitled to the privilege, they were roped off the field, where it was free of sheaves, by a rope stretched between two horses, and so carried down the field. After the corn was carried, most farmers allowed anybody to glean. The children held the ears on long stalks, in their hands close up to the heads, making neat bundles. The ears on short stems were dropped into an apron pocket.

The corn so gleaned, after being threshed, was ground at the mill free of charge and sent home to the cottages. In a good season the gleaners could usually get enough to last well through the winter.

Those cheerful gangs of hay-makers and harvesters – are they gone forever? Let us hope not. What happy and well-earned meals those were that were eaten sitting under the shady side of the hedge bank, where an oak gave wide overhead shelter.

The mower's meals were many and his wholesome drink was much, but he toiled the long day through with all the strength of his body – every muscle in full play.

Often they began work at daylight, and on some farms it was the custom that the man who came first got a pint of ale.

The mower's regular meals were: breakfast at six, lunch at half-past nine, dinner at noon, afternoon lunch at four, supper at seven, when the farmer generally gave each man a bottle of beer or cider.

A man would mow an acre of hay a day for half-a-crown or three shillings, but he could mow an acre and a half of barley. A first-rate man has mown two acres of barley. Now, an acre of hay cannot be hand-mown under ten shillings.

Gertrude Jekyll, Old West Surrey *(1904). In this book the author recorded a country way of life together with its many artefacts, which was rapidly disappearing from the county. She illustrated the book with her own photographs.*

2 · SOME QUESTIONS OF ANTIQUITY

Where did Julius Cæsar Cross the Thames?

WALTON UPON THAMES - One Simmons, a fisherman, who has lived here and known the river all his life, told the Editor in 1807, that at the place called Coway-stakes he has weighed up several stakes of the size of his thigh, about six feet long, shod with iron, the wood very black, and so hard as to turn an axe. Their boats sometimes run against them. The late Earl of Sandwich used to come to Shepperton to fish, and gave him half a guinea a-piece for some of them. There are none in any other part of the river that he ever heard of. One now remains in the river, which they were not able to weigh; it is visible when the water is clear; his net has been caught and torn by it. His tradition is, that they formed part of a bridge built by Julius Cæsar, and he describes them to have stood in two rows, as if going across the river, about nine feet asunder as the water runs, and about four feet asunder as crossing the river . . .

The tradition which has certainly prevailed for many ages that this is the place where Cæsar crossed the Thames, which is corroborated by the Camp on St. George's Hill; yet there are several learned Antiquaries who deny the fact.

Owen Manning and William Bray, The History and Antiquities of the County of Surrey *(1804-1814). Most modern archæologists agree that the camp on St. George's Hill is Iron Age not Roman.*

Roman Roads - Stane Street

Staen-Street [sic] Causeway is 10 Yards broad, but in most Places seven; two Miles and a half, or 3 Miles long: It runs from Belingsgate to Belinghurst in Sussex, and so to Arundel. It goes thro' Darking Church-yard, which they find by digging of the Graves. This Causeway is partly in Okeley Parish. In Winter 'tis extreamly wet. It is made of Flints and Pebbles; but there are no other Flints nearer than seven Miles, and the Pebbles are such as are at the Beaches in Sussex, from whence the common People say they were brought, and that it was made by the Devil: It is a Yard and a half deep in Stones, which they discover by cutting Passages to let in Water; it runs in an exact straight Line. This Way is found, by making of Ditches between Stansteed and Darking, upon the Hills. It lyes plainly to be seen in ploughed Fields, in a Farm called Monks, two Miles from hence South; and at Pulborough Heath, seven Miles on this Side Arundel; and it is seen about Newington.

John Aubrey, The Natural History and Antiquities of the County of Surrey (begun c.1673). Aubrey was incorrect to say that Stane Street went to Arundel. The section through Surrey formed part of the London to Chichester road.

Merrow Down (Just So Stories)

I

There runs a road by Merrow Down–
   A grassy track to-day it is–
An hour out of Guildford town,
   About the river Wey it is.

Here, when they heard the horse-bells ring,
   The ancient Britons dressed and rode
To watch the dark Phœnicians bring
   Their goods along the Western Road.

Yes, here, or hereabouts, they met
   To hold their racial talks and such–
To barter beads for Whitby jet,
   And tin for gay shell torques and such.

But long and long before that time
   (When bison used to roam on it)
Did Taffy and her Daddy climb
   That Down, and had their home on it.

Then beavers built in Broadstonebrook
   And made a swamp where Bramley stands;
And bears from Shere would come and look
   For Taffimai where Shamley stands.

The Wey, that Taffy called Wagai,
   Was more than six times bigger then;
And all the Tribe of Tegumai
   They cut a noble figure then!

II

Of all the Tribe of Tegumai
   Who cut that figure, none remain,
On Merrow Down the cuckoos cry–
   The silence and the sun remain.

But as the faithful years return
   And hearts unwounded sing again,
Comes Taffy dancing through the fern
   To lead the Surrey spring again.

Her brows are bound with bracken-fronds,
   And golden elf-locks fly above;
Her eyes are bright as diamonds
   And bluer than the sky above.

In mocassins and deer-skin cloak,
   Unfearing, free and fair she flits,
And lights her little damp-wood smoke
   To show her Daddy where she flits.

For far–oh, very far behind,
   So far she cannot call him,
Comes Tegumai alone to find
   The daughter that was all to him!

Rudyard Kipling (1865-1936) Works (1994 edition)

The Clue of the Grey Snail

It was at Bletchingley that I received a strange visitor, who thoroughly shook all my confidence in the generally accepted findings of the archæological world as to Roman roads and Coldharbours.

It happened this way. The good landlord of the White Hart was speeding his parting guests and closing his house for the night. We were all assembled in the quaint sitting-room of the inn, putting finishing touches to our campaign of exploration for the morning.

'A visitor to see you, Mr. Maxwell,' said mine host, as he piloted in a very tall, very thin man, strikingly like the accepted personality of Sherlock Holmes. He was dressed in dark grey, with a small cape thrown over his shoulders, and from his bicycle clips and rather dusty appearance, it was apparent that he had ridden some distance.

'Apologies for calling upon you, sir, at this hour,' he began, 'but the matter presses. I followed you here from East Farleigh.' His voice was very deep and solemn. 'I am a Watkinsian, and come to call you from the error of your ways, and from your Romeward leanings.'

I must have looked startled. There is a certain type of reformer who imagines that all people who write for the *Church Times* must have Roman leanings.

'I mean not in religion,' he continued with a grave smile, as if in answer to my thoughts, 'but in the world of England's landscape. You, with all your deduction and observation are little better than the country bumpkin who beholds Cæsar's Camp in every Celtic dun.'

I hastily ordered some drinks, found the most comfortable chair for him, introduced Scylla and Charybdis and our sapper friend – 'I did not catch your name, sir,' I said in apology.

'My name does not matter. My mission is all-important. I am a Watkinsian and a ley-hunter. You, who ought to know better, are blind as a bat concerning the old roads and tracks of England. I will make you a ley reader.'

I hastily replied that I was strict C. of E., and was not even a lay reader in that communion. Even if the Watkinsians (I must confess I had never heard of them) were in communion with the Church of England, I could not, without much further consideration of the . . .

'Not a L-A-Y reader, L-E-Y, a ley reader, a man who can read leys.

'Why are all archæologists so blind?' he continued. 'Do you not

know that when the Romans came here they found a system of roads
and tracks, properly sighted and surveyed, as old to them as the
Roman roads are to us?

'Read the leys rightly,' he went on, warming to the subject, 'and you
will see revealed the earliest history of England. Read the leys, and
you will see why our ancient parish churches are built up and down
the land in mathematical patterns. A time, long, long before the dawn
of Christianity, fixed their sites.

'Read the leys, and you will know why there are so many
Broomfields and Broom Hills where broom does not grow. Read the
leys, and you will see at once why people of old thought witches rode
on broomsticks. Read the leys, and you will know why Great
Bustington is no bigger than Little Bustington – a thing you must often
have noticed. Read the leys, and you will at last see some sense in the
stories of secret passages from one ancient place to another, often by
routes under rivers, and impossible of engineering.'

The speaker paused for breath. We broke into a murmur of
applause and admiration, though I do not think we, any of us, knew
what he was talking about. The sapper, who was sitting rather behind
the operator, gave me a look that rather suggested a wink. I am
convinced that he thought our visitor was mad. 'Er–er–awfully
interesting,' he said, 'and–er–enlightening, but–er–would you mind,
sir, telling us what a ley is?'

'A ley,' our lecturer replied, 'is an invisible and imaginary line,
drawn from one point in the landscape to another, mathematically
straight. It is not a track, though a track would often exist between
various points upon this line.

'You must not confuse a ley with a road,' he explained. 'The ley is
a direction, a line, as I have told you, invisible, and stretching across
the country from point to point.

'The key positions along these leys are points where two or more
leys cross. It will often happen, nay, at one time it generally happened,
that a track would run from one point to another on this ley. The
crossing places of these tracks would be places of meeting.

'Imagine,' he went on, 'a scattered people living in great
uncultivated regions of marsh or forest land. Here and there would be
a small clearing, probably for the convenience of communication one
with another, at various points along a ley. Imagine, too, that for some

purpose these scattered people wished to meet for purposes of exchanging goods or hearing news. What more likely place on which to meet than the mound or stone, or by the tree at the crossing of two leys which would be served by four tracks. These cross-ways would become the markets, the temple sites, or the places of stone circles of primitive times.

'I must leave you now,' he continued, 'but I will present you with this, *The Ley-Hunter's Manual*, by our great founder, Watkins, sometime president of the Woolhope Club. The discovery of the ley is a marvellous thing, and it is not yet ten years old.'

He turned to me. 'You,' he said, 'must be a ley-hunter, because you can write down what you observe, and – far more important – because you can draw what you see. Time flies. I must go. Do not come to the door, I can let myself out. I will give you two clues – without which you will do nothing. One is the Long Man of Wilmington. The other is here.'

He handed me a little wooden box, tied round with string, bowed, stalked out of the room, and was gone.

I undid the string somewhat gingerly. The box was too light to contain a bomb. At first, I thought there was nothing in it. Then something fell out, like a pebble, about half an inch in diameter.

It was a snail.

We stared in amazement, not being able to see any point in the joke, as the creature unrolled itself, and started walking across the map, which was spread out on the table before us.

'A leg-pull,' said Scylla, 'intended to indicate that you are slow in the uptake.'

'Light is beginning to dawn upon me,' said Brown. 'It is not a joke. The old English name for this snail is the dodman, and a dodman is a track surveyor with his two sticks getting an alignment. The Long Man of Wilmington is a giant figure cut in the chalk of the South Downs. It is holding a huge staff in either hand, and is a dodman.

'Our friend means that we must not guess at leys, but work them out by accurate surveying. It is a good clue – the Clue of the Grey Snail.'

Donald Maxwell, A Detective in Surrey *(1932)*.

3 · SAXONS AND NORMANS

Early Charters

In a charter dated 672-674 Frithuwold, sub-king of Surrey, granted land to Chertsey Abbey. The charter is the oldest surviving document to mention Surrey. At the end of the document Frithuwold politely suggested that anyone contravening his grant should be sent to hell!

Wherefore I, Frithuwold, of the province of the men of Surrey, sub-king of Wulfhere, king of the Mercians, of my own free will, being in sound mind and perfect understanding, from this present day grant, concede, transfer and assign from my rightful possession into yours, land for increasing the monastery which was first constructed under King Egbert, 200 hides for strengthening the same monastery, which is called Chertsey, and five hides in the place which is called Thorpe. I not only give the land, but confirm and deliver myself and my only son in obedience to Abbot Eorcenwold. And the land is, taken together, 300 hides, and moreover by the river which is called the Thames, the whole along the bank of the river as far as the boundary which is called the ancient ditch, that is Fullingdiac; again, in another part of the bank of the same river as far as the boundary of the next province, which is called Sonning. Of the same land, however, a separate part, of 10 hides, is by the port of London, where ships come to land, on the same river on the southern side of the public way. There are, however, diverse names for the above-mentioned land, namely Chertsey, Thorpe, Egham, Chobham, Getinges [in Cobham], Molesey, Woodham and Hunewaldesham [in Weybridge], as far as the above-mentioned boundary. I grant to you, Eorcenwold, and confirm it for the foundation of a monastery, that both you and your successors may be bound to intercede for the relief of my soul – along with fields, woods, meadows, pastures, and rivers and all other things duly belonging to the monastery of St Peter, Prince of Apostles, at Chertsey . . . Never, at any time, shall this charter of my donation be contravened by me or my heir. If anyone shall try to contravene this my donation and confirmation, may he be cut off from all Christian society and deprived of participation in the celestial kingdom

Dorothy Whitelock (editor), English Historical Documents c.500-1042 *(1979)*.

Kingston or Cyningeston

. . . this old market town on the Thames was a royal possession in Saxon times, when it was known as Cyningeston. It must have been of some consequence as early as 836, for it was chosen about that year for the holding of a council between Egbert and Archbishop Ceolnoth, and possibly from this meeting having taken place at Kingston it assumed the importance which made it a place of coronation for a succession of the kings of Wessex, from Athelstan in 924 to Edmund Ironside in 1016. Altogether eight kings are recorded as having been crowned here. No mention whatever is made in any historical document at present known of a coronation stone; the great topographers of the sixteenth century, Leland and Camden, make no reference to it. There was, however, in the old Chapel of St. Mary, a part of the parish church which collapsed in 1730, a large block of stone, which was afterwards removed to the outside of the Town Hall and there utilised until 1850 as a mounting block. The mayor of that time, convinced, apparently, of its antiquity and the original purpose which it had served, moved it to its present site at the cross-roads south of the market-place, and had it duly inscribed with the names of the West Saxon kings known to have been crowned at Kingston.

Gordon Home, The Charm of Surrey *(1929)*.

Murder at Guildford

In 1036 Alfred the Atheling, a claimant to the throne of England and younger brother of Edward (later to become King Edward the Confessor), arrived from Normandy and was greeted by Godwin, Earl of Wessex. Somewhere near Guildford, Godwin and his men suddenly turned from friendly hosts into vicious murderers and a horrible slaughter ensued. Here is just one of a number of versions of how Alfred met his end. It is certainly not for the faint-hearted!

Whereupon proceeding together towards London, going over Guldesdoune, the traitorous Godwin said to Alfred – 'Look around on the right hand and on the left, and behold what a realm will be subject to your dominion.' Alfred, giving thanks to God, then faithfully promised that if he should be crowned king he would institute such laws as would be pleasing and acceptable to God and men. Previously to this, Godwin had secretly given directions to his men that, in passing over Guldesdoune, they should seize Alfred and all the Normans who accompanied him and bind them. These being deceitfully captured and bound, nine out of every ten were by divers means put to death, the tenth remaining, or being left at Guldeford. But when all the Normans except one tenth of their number had been destroyed, the number left was so considerable, that the tenth first preserved was decimated, so that few escaped. For alas! Twelve gentlemen who came with Alfred from Normandy, among the rest were cruelly massacred; and Alfred, himself was deprived of his eyes at Gillingham. Then leading him to the monastery of Ely, according to some, they delivered him into the custody of the Monks, where for a short time being kept on a diet of bread, amidst unheard of torments, his miserable life terminated.

Indeed some say, that the beginning of his bowels being drawn out through an opening at his navel, and tied to a stake, he was driven in circles, with iron goads, till the latter parts of the entrails were extracted: and thus through the treachery of Godwin, Alfred died at Ely.

Abbot of Jerveaux (twelfth century).

Magna Charta

[King John's] great efforts and combinations were only frustrated by the unexpected victory of the French at Bouvines over John's troops, under the Earl of Salisbury, and over his allies, his nephew the Emperor Otto, and the Counts of Flanders and Boulogne. The defeat gave the barons in England the chance of successfully pressing their demands, which were embodied in the Great Charter. Still De Warenne remained on the King's side. There is a tradition that the barons met together in the vaults of his castle at Reigate to consider their plans, but the attitude of the lord of the castle renders this improbable, and the line of the recorded march of the baronial army brought them nowhere near Reigate. De Warenne was one of the envoys named by the King to treat with the barons, and the result of the negotiation was the greatest event which ever took place on the soil of Surrey, the signing of the Great Charter.

That the Charter was presented to and signed by the King on the soil of Surrey is nearly certain, Runimede is a meadow by the Thames, below Windsor, in the parish of Egham in Surrey. In the river lies an eyot, called Magna Charta Island, where it is usually said that the Charter was actually signed. The island is in the parish of Wraysbury in Buckinghamshire. But the Charter itself bears witness that it was given 'in prato quod vocatur Runingmede.' The name Runimede, the Mead of Council, may mark some ancient meeting-place, the memory of which was not extinct at the time, and led to the choice of the place. We may conjecture how it is that the island has been taken to have been the place of signature. The treaty by which the French Prince Louis agreed to evacuate England in 1217 was signed in an island in the Thames near Staines, according to Matthew Paris, and this island may have been that now known as Magna Charta Island, and a confusion may have arisen between the two events.

Henry Elliot Malden, A History of Surrey (1900). The signing of Magna Charta in 1215 is undoubtedly the most significant historical event to have taken place in Surrey. Although it was a settlement made only between King John and the barons, and the event did nothing to improve the lot of most Englishmen at the time, Magna Charta proved to be a major milestone upon the long road to democracy as we know it today. Unfortunately, the barons reneged on the agreement as soon as they were out of sight of Runnymede.

Castles

Four castles stood along the ridge of the Surrey downs when the barons were at war, and of the four nothing worth the name of a castle remains. Farnham's keep was broken down by Cromwell: Guildford is a shell, Reigate and Bletchingley have disappeared altogether. Betchworth, never fortified for war, was built later than the others, but Betchworth is an insignificant ruin. The kings and the captains have passed, and their buildings have followed them. The castles have gone down with the palaces. Surrey never had a castle like Arundel; but she has not been able to keep even a Pevensey or a Bodiam.

Yet Reigate castle and its owners shaped a great deal of English history. It belonged to the great Earls de Warenne, the rival family to the de Clares through all the early wars and intrigues of the kings and barons. . . Reigate Castle never saw a pitched battle. When Louis of France was riding by the ridge to Winchester after King John, Reigate surrendered to the French, and de Warenne only got his castle back by changing sides from John to Louis. That was in 1216, and forty-seven years later, when Simon de Montfort took the baron's army by the ridge to Rochester, Reigate could do no more that watch the army march by. The de Warenne of the day was at Lewes with the king, and when the king had lost all in the battle of Lewes that followed, the lord of Reigate castle fled to France. He came back the next year, and when de Montfort fell at Evesham, Reigate was once more de Warenne's.

The kings must have found this particular de Warenne a little difficult to deal with. He was a bit of a swashbuckler as well as a swordsman, and once when he found himself getting the worst of a lawsuit at Westminster with one Alan de la Zouche, he ran him through the body in the king's own chamber and was off to Reigate before anybody could stop him. King Henry was furious, and sent Prince Edward, the great de Clare, and an archbishop to bid him come out of his castle and be punished. He came out at last, and was fined ten thousand marks for the king and two thousand for Alan de la Zouche. But Prince Edward was not done with him. As Edward the First he held a Court of Assize to inquire into the warrants by which the barons held their lands. De Warenne was asked for his warrant for Reigate. He drew a rusty sword and struck it on the council table. 'By this instrument,' he said, 'do I hold my lands, and by the same I intend to keep them.' He kept them, but he had to amend his plea into something a little less swaggering.

Eric Parker, Highways and Byways in Surrey *(1908). Guildford Castle was a very sumptuous affair during the reign of Henry III in the 13th century, when it became a royal palace. Surrey also had another castle, Starborough, near Lingfield.*

4 · WILD SURREY

A Plover's Nest

Plovers' eggs in aspic may be a dainty dish, I grant, and welcomed by the gourmet, but plovers' eggs in the open field are one of the most interesting features of spring-time – that time of apple-blossom, and tree-buds and lambs – and it is heartbreaking to think that the wholesale robbery of nests is fast leading to the extinction of this popular and handsome British bird.

Housewives, think for a moment before writing out your menu! It is only want of thought on your part. When you think of plucking the feathers from your hats let the eggs bide in the nest!

A walk up a red Surrey lane in April with open eyes for Nature's most perfect beauties discovers many treasures hidden from those who go blindfold through this beautiful world . . .

. . . To find a peewit's nest, on the contrary, is anything but an easy task, except to an expert. I crept quietly into the ploughed field. Overhead a lark was singing lustily, and on the brow a covey of red-legged partridges scuttled out of sight.

Then a plover arose and began to turn somersaults in the air, crying over and over again, 'Pee-wit . . . weet. Weet. Pee-weet . . . weet, weet,' and flapping his wings wildly, producing the noise like the humming of a top or the striking of a violin string with the finger.

This, of course, was the male bird doing his level best to keep all the attention to himself; and he can hardly fail in his endeavour, for it is marvellous what antics these birds go through on the wing.

They dart upwards as if the sky itself was their goal, then, as if afraid of the sunlight, they suddenly sweep downwards, describing an 'abrupt and wavy course with many turnings.' Down almost to the ground at the intruder's feet, then up again to turn over and over in a wild sky dance.

All the while the cry is incessant, and the beating of the long pinions becomes louder and louder.

It was all to no effect. A quick eye detected a mother bird silently leave her next, her grey crest clear against the skyline, and after running along a furrow fly silently over the thorn hedge into the next field.

Then the search began, backwards and forwards, carefully, and for a long time fruitlessly. Soon a friendly shepherd left his flock and crossed the plough.

'I'll show you the nest,' he said, and after a moment's search, and a long pause, 'but you've nearly done for it this time;' and he showed me two footmarks, one on either side of the nest, where in the search I had made I had crossed the very nest itself.

A few stray bents laid carefully in a slight depression of the ground forms the peewit's home, and on this scanty surface lie the four dark olive-green eggs spotted with black, arranged crosswise, the four points touching each other in the centre.

These eggs soon get dusted with the brown earth, and of course this makes them still more difficult to find.

I bade the shepherd guard the eggs as he would guard his flock, and a grin acknowledged the promise of a reward if the eggs were hatched instead of being landed in aspic.

The 'sounding flight and wailing cry' of the distressed male bird soon awoke another parent, and yet another, and soon five birds were wheeling away in the air overhead. But the first mother did not join the wild dance. She watched silently with a beating heart behind the hedge, and she only slipped back to her nest when the enemy left the field.

Over and over again the same nest was revisited, and each time the same scene was witnessed, the mother bird leaving silently and reappearing again, as if by magic, when the coast was clear. Perhaps the male bird in the air gave her some sign as he repeated 'Pee-weet . . . weet, weet' in a minor key.

At last, during one visit, a glance at the bottom of the field revealed to me horses and men, and a sowing machine. Corn was being cast on the soft brown earth. This was an unforeseen danger. If the peewits were to be saved they must break the shell and run. Luckily baby peewits run very soon after they emerge from the shell.

It was the fifteenth day, so if only men and horse walk slow, or a kindly shower stays the work, my birds will be safe.

When I found the nest, with ever the same difficulty, three eggs were there, and in place of the fourth a flat black body was visible.

Louder and louder wailed the father in the air, as he turned over and swept up and down in a perfect rage of anxiety.

Surely the birdlet was dead? But a gently poke with my finger produced a diminutive *piano* 'pee-weet', a faint baby cry for his mother's warmth.

Then one of the other eggs moved, and the beak of an imprisoned birdlet gave a brave peck, and through the window of shell a second baby 'dixhuit' took his first glance out into a great unknown, cold, endless world. 'Pee-weet . . .weet, weet' screamed his father, and I thought it best to beat a hasty retreat, for it is just as a bird leaves the shell that the mother is most sorely needed.

We read that sixty years ago, in one season, and from one marsh alone, two hundred dozen plovers' eggs were taken, and today the birds are far more scarce, and yet the eggs are persistently taken and persistently eaten.

'There used to be twenty thur in that field,' grumbled an old weatherbeaten man as the lane was reached. 'You ca' tell when a bird gets up whether 'e'd got eggs or whether 'e 'adnt,' he went on moodily. 'there's a deal o' people about now, there is.' And with this parting shot he returned to his work.

At once the plovers ceased calling, for the intruders were out of sight. Of course the ideal lapwing would have led us out of the gate, feigning a broken wing or leg, but the real peewit only wails overhead, and fantastically twists and turns.

Helen Millman, Outside the Garden *(1900). The author lived at Tilford.*

Tempest and Flood at Kingston

Thursday at nyght rose a great winde and rayne that the Temps rosse so hye that they myght row with botts owte of the Temps a gret waye in to the market place and upon a sodayne.

Kingston Parish Register, 9th October 1570.

The Great Storm of 1703

26 Nov 1703. The dismall Effects of the Hurecan & Tempest of Wind, raine & lightning thro all the nation, especial London, many houses demolished, many people killed: & as to my owne losse, the subversion of Woods & Timber both left for Ornament, and Valuable materiall thro my whole Estate, & about my house, the Woods crowning the Garden Mount, & growing along the Park meadow; the damage to my owne dwelling, & Tennants farmes & Outhouses is most Tragicall: not to be paralleled with any thing hapning in our Age in any history almost.

The Diary of John Evelyn, edited by E.S. de Beer (1959). Evelyn's estate was at Wotton. It was in 1987 that a severe storm again wrought havoc in Surrey.

The Thames

Sir John Denham lived at Egham and the first version of his poem, 'Cooper's Hill', was published in 1642. A much revised edition appeared in 1655. His inspiration came from the views, particularly of the Thames, that the poet saw from the hill near his home.

> O could I flow like thee, and make thy stream
> My great example, as it is my theme.
> Though deep, yet clear, though gentle, yet not dull;
> Strong without rage, without o'erflowing full.
> Thames, the most loved of all the ocean's sons,
> By his old sire, to his embrace runs;
> Hasting to pay his tribute to the sea,
> Like mortal life to meet eternity.

Sir John Denham (1615-1669), an extract from 'Cooper's Hill' (1655).

Violent Storm at Richmond

There happened on Whitsunday, May 21, 1711, in the Afternoon, at this place, an Accident by Thunder and Lightning very surprizing, and very terrible, especially to those that were nearest it. At about half an Hour past Three of the Clock, when it had sometime before Thundered and Lightened at a distance, which was attended with Rain and a pretty high Wind, on a sudden there came a violent Clap, which fell upon a Brick-Building, distinct from any House, consisting of two Stables, and two Coach-Houses, over which were Hay-lofts and Rooms for Servants to lie in. The Lightning and Clap of Thunder came all at once, there being not any Space of Time betwixt the one and the other, as is usual when at a greater Distance, but it resembled the discharge of a Cannon, when a Person stands very near it. Take the following Account of the Effects of this Storm upon the Front of this Building, which is to the North-East; and first, The Glass Windows were broken, shattered, and burst outwards; the Brick-work was broken and pierced, but not through, except one little Hole; the Corner of the Window-Frame was struck through, as if 'twas done by a small Cannon-Ball, and shivered to Pieces. Two more Places in the Brick-work were broken, and two small Holes quite through; at the lower-most of which, within the Bricks, it was more torn than without, and thrown all over the Room. There was left a black Mark of Sulphur, which fixed itself on the Beam and one of the Coach-house Doors. There were three young Men, Apprentices to Watermen at Twittenham, who coming by at the Time of the Storm, stood up under this Building for Shelter; one of them was found Dead upon the Spot, with the Coach-house Door upon him; but whether that or the Lightning was the Occasion of his Death, is uncertain; 'tis supposed the latter, because he bled at one Ear; the Hair of the back Part of his Head, and of his Beard, was singed, and the Blood settled round his Neck. The other two young Men were both wounded by the Lightning on one side of the Belly, and down one Thigh. One of them crawl'd away and got immediate Help, and was likely to do well; but the other was found gasping for Life on the Dunghill, but was somewhat recovered by being let Blood, &c. however, he did not live.

John Aubrey, The Natural History and Antiquities of the County of Surrey (begun c.1673). Once again the then popular cure of blood-letting probably finished off the second victim!

A Springtime Walk in a Surrey Lane

The tiny white petals of the barren strawberry open under the April sunshine which, as yet unchecked by crowded foliage above, can reach the moist banks under the trees. It is then that the first stroll of the year should be taken in Claygate Lane. The slender runners of the strawberries trail over the mounds among the moss, some of the flowers but just above the black and brown leaves of last year which fill the shallow ditch. These will presently be hidden under the grass which is pushing up long blades, and bending over like a plume.

Crimson stalks and leaves of herb Robert stretch across the little cavities of the mound; lower, and rising almost from the water of the ditch, the wild parsnip spreads its broad fan. Slanting among the underwood, against which it leans, the dry white 'gix' (cow-parsnip) of last year has rotted from its root, and is only upheld by branches.

Yellowish green cup-like leaves are forming upon the brown and drooping heads of the spurge, which, sheltered by the bushes, has endured the winter's frosts. The lads pull them off, and break the stems, to watch the white 'milk' well up, the whole plant being full of acrid juice. Whorls of woodruff and grass-like leaves of stitchwort are rising; the latter holds but feebly to the earth, and even in snatching the flower the roots sometimes give way and the plant is lifted with it.

Richard Jefferies, Nature near London *(1883). The author lived at Tolworth, just a short distance from Claygate Lane. He died in 1887, aged 38.*

Rusticus

The observations of nature made by 'Rusticus' were brought together in the book Letters of Rusticus. *The real name of the writer has never been indisputably confirmed but is thought by many to have been Edward Newman, who came to live in Godalming in 1817. The author was an observant countryman and pioneer naturalist, as this short piece clearly illustrates.*

When the lengthening days give the first impulse to the feathered tribes to bend their course northward for the breeding season, it is here that I listen for the first notes of the chiffchaff; here I watch for the blackcap, the nightingale, the willow-wrens, the garden warblers,

the white-throat; here, hour after hour, have I hunted for their nests, my object not being plunder, but information. Often have I covered my hand with scratches, from the prickles of briars and brambles, in my attempts to gain a satisfactory view of a nest and its contents without causing any disarrangement, well knowing how great was the risk of desertion if the parent birds should discover anything amiss; and, when deserted, if I knew not the builders, a nest was valueless. How well was I repaid for bleeding hands, if I discovered but one point in the history of the species. Eggs strung on bents are rife in all country places; old nests are easy to be seen when the leaves are gone; birds are plentiful in every hedge-row, and their song is the burthen of the passing breeze: but to connect with certainty each bird with its mate; to assign it the proper nest and proper eggs; to learn the exact time of its arrival and its departure; – all this is a study, a labour, rarely undertaken, and affords a pleasure akin to that which must be felt by a traveller exploring countries where man has not before trodden.
Letters of Rusticus *(1849)*.

Summer Voices

Denham Jordan wrote several books in the latter part of the nineteenth century about the countryside and wildlife under the pen name of 'A Son of the Marshes'. Although Kent born, he spent much of his life in the Dorking area of Surrey.

Just now the woods and the fields that surround them are never still; by day or night the pulse of Nature beats audibly.

It is mid-summer in the woodlands, and so hot is it that the seed-pods of the furze bushes pop and crack, the seeds sowing themselves in all directions, Nature being her own seed-distributor. The lizards stretch themselves on the bare stones out in the open, or climb to the very top shoots of the furze bushes, inflating their throats, apparently from the pure joy of existence. It is hot, but this is life-giving heat; and there are various kinds of heat – one will take all the life out of you, whilst another will make you feel, as our old folks say, 'as brisk as a bumble-bee in a tar-pot.'

The simile is not a bad one; insects are attracted by scent. When bees, the common hive-bees, are on the wing, although none to your certain knowledge may be near you, if you melt a bit of bee's-wax in an iron ladle and wave it about, in less than twenty minutes you will have your place swarming with hive-bees. So well is this fact known in the country, though it be in the middle of summer, all the windows and doors are closed.

As you look up through all the greenery of the woods, you can see the leaves on the very topmost shoots quiver. Where does the air come from, for we can feel no wind stir?

When we gain the crest of the hill crowned by a clump of firs, a noticeable feature of our Surrey hills, we rest for a time. All is still; there is not enough air, so far as it can be felt, to deviate the course of one falling fir-needle. But in the air above us the summer voice of the firs is whispering. The voices of the trees change with the seasons; just now they speak in a dreamy monologue of undertones.

The birds know in some mysterious way that this is the time for them to renew their strength after their arduous maternal duties. In the bright spring-time the wood-pigeon – the 'cushat-doo' – could give full vent to all the exuberance of his vitality. He crooned to his mate, rose in the air, spread out his tail, inflated his neck, and clapped his wings above his back so loudly and frequently for her admiration.
Now, as we look up through the heavy dark-green tracery, we can see them both sitting side by side in a kind of Darby-and-Joan fashion. The land itself must rest. There are seed-time and harvest, and the rest-time of fallow lands; this is an imperative law of Nature, carried out by all created beings.

You can see the creatures that the woods hold by fits and starts only; for they know that a man is in their haunts, and they come in their quiet manner to find out if he intends them harm. Recently a squirrel ate his provender just over my head, and the fawn-backed, white-bellied, large-eyed wood-mouse, or, as he is called from his love of cultivation, the garden-mouse, sat up on his haunches and trimmed his fine long whiskers almost at my feet. The two great problems of life and death follow quickly on each other, for hardly had the little fellow gone when one of his most determined enemies, in the shape of a weasel, made his appearance, looked at me with his bold dark eyes, and then followed on the track of the mouse.

The southern slopes of hills are naturally preferred by all creatures furred or feathered, and our road home will lead us to descend in that direction. Now and again we come on bare places where huge beech-trees have been felled for timber. Before the remains in the shape of 'lop' and 'top' are cleared off, a crop of vegetation never seen before springs up like magic; one of the magical workings of the woodlands this is. To these newly opened spaces the larger species of the fritillaries are singularly attracted.

Travellers in tropical countries have mentioned a distinct sound made in flight by some of the tropical species. The Queen of Spain fritillary, and the high brown fritillary, and also the silver-washed fritillary, when on flight, click with their strong wings. This I have heard distinctly as the grand creatures have flown within a yard of me. So quiet at times are these open spots, that a beetle can be heard running or crawling over the dead leaves. When the sun dips down, then is the time to hear summer voices.

'A Son of the Marshes', From Spring to Fall (1894).

An Early Sighting of the Surrey Puma?

On many occasions in recent years there have been reports of the appearance at various localities in Surrey of an animal of feline shape which, however, appeared to be considerably larger then a normal domestic moggy. In the 1970s 'experts' suggested there could be an escaped puma at large in the county, but such mysterious beasts seem to have been around for quite a time!

We came hither by the way of Waverley Abbey and Moore Park . . . I showed him a tree, close by the ruins of the Abbey, from a limb of which I once fell into the river, in an attempt to take the nest of a crow, which had artfully placed it upon a branch so far from the trunk as not to be able to bear the weight of a boy eight years old. I showed him an old elm tree, which was hollow even then, into which I, when a very little boy, once saw a cat go, that was as big as a middle-sized spaniel dog, for relating which I got a great scolding, for standing to which I, at last, got a beating; but stand to which I still did. I have since many times repeated it; and I would take my oath of it to this day. When in New Brunswick I saw the great wild grey cat, which is there called a Lucifee; and it seemed to me to be just such a cat as I had seen at Waverley.

William Cobbett, Rural Rides (1830).

Lines Written at Box Hill

*George Meredith, poet and novelist, made his home at Flint Cottage,
Box Hill, one of the county's most popular beauty spots.*

Lovely are the curves of the white owl sweeping
    Wavy in the dusk lit by one large star,
Lone on the fir-branch, his rattle-note unvaried
    Brooding o'er the gloom, spins the brown evejar.
Darker grows the valley, more and more forgetting:
    So were it with me if forgetting could be willed.
Tell the grassy hollow that holds the bubbling well-spring,
    Tell it to forget the source that keeps it filled.

George Meredith (1828-1909), Love in a Valley.

5 · THE TOWNS

Croydon

In a house like that
    Your Uncle Dick was born;
Satchel on back he walked to Whitgift
    Every weekday morn.

Boys together in Coulsdon Woods
    Bramble-berried and steep,
He and his pals would look for spadgers
    Hidden deep.

The laurels are speckled in Marchmont Avenue
    Just as they were before,
But the steps are dusty that still lead up to
    Your Uncle Dick's front door.

Pear and apple in Croydon gardens
    Bud and blossom and fall,
But your Uncle Dick has left his Croydon
    Once for all.

John Betjeman, Collected Poems *(1966).*

Epsom

July 15th [1797], London to Epsom, in Surrey, 16 miles. The people busy mowing and making hay, and much grass yet to cut, which I thought rather singular at this time of the year, and so near the metropolis. In this day's journey I crossed a common, occupied with furze and a few ill-looking sheep; a sight I little thought to have met with in this enlightened part of the country; and on travelling a little farther, I was still more convinved of my ill-founded ideas as to agricultural improvement in these southern climes: I passed over a very extensive common field, where the naturally fertile soil is exhausted by constant cropping. The surface of this district is pretty level, but not without some easy swells. A great many elm-trees grow on the hedges; elm seems to be the principal sort of wood attended to, both in this county and Essex. It is a knotty, and, in my opinion, far from being the most serviceable species of timber, either for building or farming purposes; the knots, however, seem to be produced by an injudicious practice, which prevails here, of lopping off the branches. Sheep are a long-horned white faced and legged breed, and in shape somewhat resembling those of Norfolk. Buildings are generally made of brick and tile, and almost every cottage has a vine or two spread along the walls, which produced grapes often in abundance. Great neatness seems to be observed about the houses and gardens; in and near the latter, there appears to be a taste for having pieces of water, overlooked by weeping willows and occupied by various and curious sorts of fish, swans, &c. Epsom is an extremely pleasant well-built town, surrounded with good land, pretty fields, and plenty of trees, without being an incumbrance. Here I spent two or three days in the most agreeable manner, at the house of the Rev. J. Boucher, rector of this place. The elegant house, gardens, and pleasure grounds occupied by this gentleman, are his own property, and are planned with a degree of taste and neatness not often equalled: his collection of plants is large, and curious; and besides all the common sorts of fruit, there is scarcely a wall which does not support the spreading vine, covered with clusters of grapes.

Mr Houseman's Tour of England *(1797), a cutting from an unidentified magazine.*

Egham

Another mile and a half and Bell Weir Lock is reached, where the river Colne, which forms the boundary between Buckinghamshire and Middlesex, falls into the Thames. Here the rain fortunately ceased, so we left the Fuzzy-Wuzzy at the boathouse and made across the fields direct for Egham, a pretty little town in Surrey lying perhaps half a mile from the river bank . . . We sallied forth to see what of interest Egham possesses for the stranger. It was not much that we found.

Henry Wellington Wack, In Thamesland *(1906). The* Fuzzy-Wuzzy *was a fifteen foot canoe.*

Redhill

Redhill town has not existed long enough to have accumulated any history. When the more direct route was made this way, avoiding Reigate, in 1816, Redhill was – a hill. The hill is still here, as the cyclist well enough knows, and we will take on trust that red gravel whence its name comes; but since that time the town of Redhill, now numbering some 16,000 persons, has come into existence, and when we speak of Redhill we mean – not the height up which the coaches laboured, but a certain commonplace town lying at the foot of it, with a busy railway junction where there are always plenty of trains, but never the one you want, and quite a number of public institutions of the asylum and reformatory type.

The railway junction has, of course, created Redhill town, which, is really in the parish of Reigate. When the land began to be built upon, in the '40's, it was called 'Warwick Town,' after the then Countess of Warwick, the landowner, and the names of a road and a public-house still bear witness to that somewhat lickspittle method of nomenclature. But there is, and can be, only one possible Warwick in England, and 'Redhill' this 'Warwick Town,' by natural selection, became.

There could have been no more certain method of inviting the most odious of comparisons than that of naming Redhill after the fine old feudal town of Warwick, which first arose beneath the protecting walls of its ancient castle. Either town has an origin typical of its era, and both look their history and circumstances. Redhill, within the memory of those still living, sprang up around a railway platform, and the only object that may be said to frown in it is the great gas-holder, built on absolutely the most prominent and desirable site in the whole town; and that not only frowns, but stinks as well, and is therefore not a desirable substitute for a castle keep.

Charles G. Harper, The Brighton Road *(1906).*

Farnham

Farnham, like Guildford, covers more ground than it covered five years ago – much more than it covered ten years ago. Prosperity dresses in red, and Farnham must be more prosperous than before; so prosperous, indeed, that a year or two ago it was able to contemplate without regret the possible loss or destruction of the Jolly Farmer Inn, which the tradition of more than a century asserts to have been the house in which Cobbett was born. One part of Farnham, at all events, felt able to bear that loss, and asked with some asperity for proof instead of tradition; but tradition, surely, is good enough in a place which has always been proud of Cobbett, and of which, as his birthplace, Cobbett himself was proud. He must have shown the house in which he was born to others besides his son Dick, and others must have talked about it more than Dick did. Dick, as we know from 'Rural Rides,' when he was shown the house, 'pulled up his horse and looked very hard at it, but said nothing.' Still, he looked hard at it.

Does prosperity mean another change at Farnham? Prosperity, I suppose, brought the Bank, which spoils Castle Street; and perhaps the sound of the till is preferable to other sounds. At all events, Farnham hears less of other sounds. When I began this paper I wanted to hear again the Farnham chimes, which have always remained with me as the very spirit of the place, ever since I first heard them in the fields between the church and the Wey. So I came to town on a September evening, and went through the churchyard to the familiar path through the fields, and waited for six o'clock to strike. Six o'clock struck, and no more. I waited; perhaps I had forgotten some interval between the hour and the chimes. But it was soon plain that I had forgotten nothing. There were two answers to questions I asked:

one was that 'they take them off sometimes, when there's a service or anything' (but there was no service); the other was that if you lived in West Street you would be grateful when the chimes were not ringing, because keeping on so long every three hours, morning, noon, and night, was too much of a good thing altogether. And that, no doubt, is a point of view much more easy for a resident than a visitor to realize. But if the chimes get that welcome from West Street, the end is in sight – unless, indeed, there could be another end. Chimes at night miss their pupose; but if they can be timed to ring every three hours, why not at other intervals? Why not twice a day, at noon and at six o'clock only? At six o'clock they would distrurb West Street very little, and at six o'clock visitors could listen to them. West Street may be assured that the chimes have brought visitors before now, twice and three times; they have brought me more often than that, and they brought me last September – to listen to West Street.

Eric Parker writing in the introduction to A West Surrey Sketch-book *by William Hyde (1913). I think the residents of West Street won the day!*

Richmond

There are balls at Richmond Wells every Monday and Thursday during the summer. There are men of all professions and religion, so that, be one's inclination what it may, you will find one's stamp to converse with. If you will make love, a stranger is everywhere welcome. At play they will be a deal too cunning for you, and for drinking, you may be matched night and morning. In short, for a man of no business, whose time hangs on his hand, commend me to Richmond.

Daniel Defoe, A Journey through England *(1724).*

Godalming

Godalming is a rarity among English country towns in that it has no central open space of any sort. There are simply three narrow curving streets meeting at the Market Hall. Perhaps the explanation is that Guildford is only four miles away and that Godalming had been an industrial town (cloth-making) rather than a rural centre. This does not sound an inspired town plan; in fact it is transformed by the quality of the Market Hall, a shapely, smooth early C 19 stucco building with an open arcaded ground floor subtly placed so that the curving views are always led through the 'outdoor room' under the market hall and tantalizingly around the corner. The perspectives change continuously as one walks on: the only point of rest, and a delightful one, is under the Market Hall itself.

Ian Nairn and Nikolaus Pevsner, The Buildings of England: Surrey, *2nd edition (1971).*

Darking or Dorking

This town is situated upon a Rock of soft sandy Stone, wherein are several convenient Cellars digged, both pleasant and profitable. The adjacent Fields are a sandy Soil, hot and dry; the Paving of the Town in the Year 1649, hath added much to the Handsomeness thereof. Here is, a little below, a Stream of running Water, supplied by several Springs and deep Wells. The Market is on Thursday; the Fair is on Ascension-Day; and is most Days furnished with all Sorts of Sea-fish.

John Aubrey, The Natural History and Antiquities of the County of Surrey.

Guildford

Guildford is now a large bustling place with many new streets and houses, among which are embedded a few fragments of the ancient town. Unfortunately some of these are considered obstacles in the path of modern civilisation hurrying to nowhere in particular, but demanding insistently that everything shall be cleared out of the way.

Perhaps the situation of the town in olden times did lend some colour to the legend still nursed by local patriotism that this is the Astolat of Arthurian days, the home of the lily maid, and the castle that which Launcelot saw 'Fired from the west, far on a hill.'

Once only I saw the castle glowing like that in the setting sun, as Tennyson may have seen it, but to place the legend in this spot is like trying to localise a dream.

James S. Ogilvy, A Pilgrimage in Surrey, Vol. 1 *(1914).*

7 . GOOD CHEER

Guildford Inns

Guildford: this town hath very faire Innes and good entertainment at the Tavernes, the Angell, the White Hart, the Crowne, and the Lyon.
John Taylor known as 'the Water Poet' writing in 1636.

Aug. 7, 1688, Came at night to Guildford where the Red Lion was so full of people, and a wedding, that the master of the house did get us lodging over the way, at a private house, his landlord's, mighty neat and fine, and then supped, and so to bed.
Samuel Pepys, Diary.

The accommodation here is probably the best in England; the Red Lion can make fifty beds; the White Hart not quite so big, but has more noble rooms.
John Aubrey, The Natural History and Antiquities of the County of Surrey, *(begun c.1673).*

Illegal Beer at Dorking

Thomas Bothill of Dorking brewer, 1 Dec. 1661, sold and uttered there three barrels of strong beer for other than domestic use to William Woonham victualler who then sold and uttered it as a common alehouse-keeper or tippler having no licence.
Surrey Quarter Sessions, January 1662.

Short Measures in Ewell

Joseph Reeves of Ewell Inholder [was charged] for selling Ale in a Pott for a Quart which wants of its due measure halfe a pinte 20th November last past and also for keeping game in his house att Cards and Dice.
General Sessions held at Croydon, January 1690.

The Marquis of Granby, Dorking

'You may go, Sam,' said Mr. Pickwick.

'Thank'ee, sir,' replied Mr. Weller; and having made his best bow, and put on his best clothes, Sam planted himself on the top of the Arundel coach, and journeyed on to Dorking.

The Marquis of Granby, in Mrs. Weller's time, was quite a model of a road-side public-house of the better class – just large enough to be convenient, and small enough to be snug.

On the opposite side of the road, was a large sign-board on a high post, representing the head and shoulders of a gentleman with an apoplectic countenance, in a red coat with deep blue facings, and a touch of the same blue over his three-cornered hat, for a sky. Over that again, were a pair of flags; beneath the last button of his coat were a couple of cannon; and the whole formed an expressive and undoubted likeness of the Marquis of Granby of glorious memory.

The bar window displayed a choice collection of geranium plants, and a well-dusted row of spirit phials. The open shutters bore a variety of golden inscriptions, eulogistic of good beds and neat wines; and the choice group of countrymen and hostlers lounging about the stable-door and horse-trough, afforded presumptive proof of the excellent quality of the ale and spirits which were sold within. Sam Weller paused, when he dismounted from the coach, to note all these little indications of a thriving business, with the eye of an experienced traveller; and having done so, stepped in at once.

Charles Dickens, Pickwick Papers. *There is still debate over Dickens's model for the inn, as there was no 'Marquis of Granby' situated in Dorking.*

An East Clandon Pub Rat

In an old work on rural sports published in 1813, it is stated that in 1812 a rat was killed in East Clandon, near Guildford. It measured from the tip of the nose to the end of the tail two feet, three inches, and was of proportionate bulk. It is supposed it had infested the cellar, where caught, for years, and the landlord calculates it had drunk about a barrel of beer out of the tap tub, and eaten upwards of a bushel of bread, besides a quantity of other provisions. Wonderful rat! *Reported in the* Surrey Magazine, *July 1903.*

The Battle of the Decanters

Kingston-on-Thames has been moved to its inmost depths. Kingston can sometimes be noisy and even riotous. But in the dead season, when there are no boating-men dawdling about the river-side inns, the old place wears a sleepy aspect, a grey, time-worn look, and passive as the ancient King's Stone itself, that, railing engirdled, rests in the market-square. Of late, however, Kingston-on-Thames has been wide-awake – for the winter time. It has had municipal affairs to settle. Its mayor and corporation have had a rough bout. The people of Kingston are divided on the subject of corporate Sunday tippling. As thus. On the second Sunday in each succeeding month it is the custom of his worship the mayor, attended by members of the council, to visit the parish church in semi-state. On these occasions wine is offered to the members of the council both before and after church, before church to give them strength to endure the ordeal, and afterwards to recruit their constitutions shattered with the strain of the service. To take wine with comfortable elegance it is – the opinion of the late Lord Brudenell notwithstanding – necessary to have decanters. And such decanters and their accompanying wine glasses were the cause of Kingston-on-Thames having been divided against itself. At a late meeting of the town council, when the quarterly accounts came up for consideration, there arose a stern conscript father and denounced an item of eighty-nine shillings for decanters and wine glasses ordered by his worship the mayor for the purposes of the corporation as already described. The wordy war raged long and loud, and in the end the decanters had it, though not before a bold churchman had declared that the opposition to the item only came from dissenters, who, because they did not go to church, had none of the wine. Spectators declare the battle of the decanters to have been a stirring fray, the good burghers of Kingston fighting for their ancient privileges to the last drop.

Surrey Advertiser, 10th February, 1877.

The Swan Inn, Thames Ditton

The Swan, snug inn, good fare affords,
As table e'er was put on
And worthy quite of grander boards
Is poultry, fish and mutton:
And while sound wines my host supplies,
With beer of Meux and Tritton,
Mine hostess with her bright blue eyes,
Invites to stay at Ditton

Theodore Hook (1788-1841), Written on a Wine-glass.

Crutchless Old Enjoy the Inn

At an entertainment given by the master of the Talbot-Inn, at Ripley, in Surry [sic], on Shrove Tuesday last, to twelve of the neighbours, inhabitants of the said parish, the age of the whole amounted to one thousand and eighteen years: what is still more remarkable, one of the company is the mother of twelve children, the youngest of whom is sixty; she has within this fortnight walked to Guildford and back again, which is twelve miles, in one day: another has worked as a journeyman with his master (a shoemaker, who dined with him) forty-nine years: they all enjoyed their senses, and not one made use of a crutch.

Annual Register, 1759.

Dorking Inns, Water-souchy and Cherry Wine

A century ago the inns here derived some of their importance from a custom which had then been long prevalent of selling corn in them on market days, the wheat being lodged in the public-houses for this purpose. Among the leading hostelries, the 'King's Head' was, early in the present century [19th], celebrated for fish-river[sic] dinners, in which water-souchy formed a prominent dish.

Here, in a footnote, the writer gives a recipe for water-souchy:

As few people appear to be acquainted with the composition of water-souchy, the receipt for the concoction of this dish is here given from a *Cookery Book*, 'by a Lady,' published in 1833, p.18:-

'Stew two or three flounders, some parsley roots and leaves, thirty peppercorns, and a quart of water, till the fish are boiled to pieces; pulp them through a sieve. Set over the fire the pulped fish, the liquor that boiled them, some perch, tench, or flounders, and some fresh roots or leaves of parsley; simmer all till done enough, then serve in a deep dish. Slices of bread and butter are to be sent to table to eat with the souchy.

. . . Whilst on the subject of inns, it may be noted that a writer, in 1750, says of Surrey: 'There is also a kind of wild Black Cherry, that grows about Dorking, of which the inhabitants make considerable quantities of Red Wine, much wholsomer and but little inferior to French Claret.'

J. Lewis André, Miscellaneous Antiquities of Dorking, *Surrey Archæological Collections Vol. 14 (1899). The perch and tench were caught from the River Mole nearby, and several other writers suggest a version of water-souchy made entirely from the local perch.*

Lunch at the Bull

Limpsfield is rather less than a mile and a half away – the outlying houses can be seen from Titsey. After following the road a short distance, the visitor can strike into the fields on the left, and make his way to the church. This, again, is totally unlike the other churches we have passed – evidently the church of a large parish, with the graveyard covered with tombstones, among them a stone near the wall of the church, with a staring coat of arms engraved on it. There are few places in which the mummery of heraldry could seem more absurd. An old manor house nearly opposite the church south, was once, according to Murray's *Guide*, 'occupied by the widow of Philip Stanhope, the natural son of Lord Chesterfield, whose well-known letters to her husband were published by Mrs Stanhope after his death.' In the upper part of the village street are one or two small shops and the 'Bull Inn,' whither I made haste to go for a frugal lunch. I found a notice inside the little bar (which is only about half as large again as the painted Bull on the sign-post outside) making public the important fact that 'parriffen oil' could be obtained there at 2s per gallon; but this, although tempting, was not quite what I was in search of. You cannot make a really good lunch on 'parriffen oil.' Ultimately I succeeded in getting some bread and cheese, and while I was working my way through a 'hunch' of dry bread, an old man came in and called for a glass of stout. He was one of the cross-grained scandal-mongering persons who seem so common in rural villages – full of ill-natured gossip and sour remarks. Presently I managed to get into conversation with him by asking him if that was not a very old house just opposite the inn?

'Hold?' said he. 'Yes, and it might do well enough for a hofficer's widow or a hold parson as ain't no use, but it ain't fit for a human being to live in as is of any account.'

Not being quite prepared for this outburst against an inoffensive looking house, I said nothing. But the landlady, who was wiping a glass, interposed: 'Account, indeed? you are letting your tongue wag pretty free to-day, I think.'

'Well, this is a free country, ain't it? Ain't it, sir?' turning to me.
'I have always understood so,' said I, not wishing to commit myself too far before so slashing a critic.

'May I make bold to ask what brings you out in this here out-o'-the-way place, sir?'

'I want to see some churches.'

'Well, well!' looking at me curiously, as if I were an escaped lunatic.

'We has artists down here sometimes – I know they are poor, and I don't believe they are over honest. But I never seed a gent as wasn't an artist going about looking at churches. As for being poor, I don't mind that. Gi' me a poor man anytime of day rather than a rich one.'

'Then you live in a world where you can be very easily accommodated.'

'I tell you what it is,' said this old man, thumping his fist on the bar, 'the rich are too stuck up, and I want to see 'em took down. They throw a word to you when they do speak as if they throwed a bone to a dog. Look at Mr. – (mentioning a name). Why you'd think he was made of some better kind of stuff than you are.'

'I don't know that he is not,' I said; 'perhaps he is.'

'I know what I'd do if I were young enough – I'd get away from 'em all, and emigrate to Canady or Horsetralia, where one man is as good as another. Everybody is rich over there, or leastways it's their own fault if they ain't.'

'But,' said I, 'I thought you did not like the rich? You don't mean to tell me you want to belong to them yourself?'

'You are getting into a mess,' said the landlady.

'That's my business if I am,' growled the man. 'I'm not rambling around pretending to look at churches. I can pay for what I have, I can.'

Evidently I was becoming a prey to the local satirist, and therefore I went on munching my bread and cheese in silence. 'Would I stand some beer?' said my acquaintance, presently. No, I would not do that, but I offered to treat him to a yeoman's draught of 'parriffen oil,' for all the other liquors he had evidently had enough and to spare. But he did not care for that, and soon I went on my way in peace.

Louis J. Jennings, Field Paths and Green Lanes, 4th edition (1884).

Lord Macaulay Visits an Alehouse

I was walking from Esher to Ditton Marsh and a shower came on. Afraid for my chest, I turned into a small alehouse, and called for a glass of ginger beer. I found there a party of hop-pickers come back from the neighbourhood of Farnham. They had had but a bad season, and were returning, walked off their legs. I liked their looks, and thought their English remarkably good for their rank of life. It was in truth Surrey English. The people had a foaming hot pot before them; but as soon as they heard the price, they rose, and were going to leave it untouched. They could not, they said, afford so much. It was but fourpence halfpenny. I laid the money down, and their delight and gratitude quite affected me.

Lord Macauley (1800-1859) Letters.

The Bear at Esher

The first animated being we encountered was a majestic and venerable raven, which immediately turned back and preceded us to 'The Brown Bear,' drawing innumerable corks by the way, as though possessed of instinctive knowledge of what our thirsty throats were panting for.

'The Brown Bear' is a capital inn, prettily situated, pretty in itself, and pretty extensive; and the raven's leading us there was a triumph of animal sagacity over human reason, for Ned had strenuously recommended us to patronise 'The White Lion,' where he had once slept for a week, but which is little better than a pot-house, and, though kept by respectable people, is far from pleasant or inviting. Its charm in Ned's eyes was, of course, cheapness; but Mr. Bang declaring it was 'cheap and nasty,' he was overruled.

The favourable impression we conceived of 'The Bear' has since been several times confirmed, as Ned and I and a party of friends annually make it a half-way house to 'the Derby.' Our plan is for some of us to go down the evening before, and sleep there, have a game of quoits, and a ramble on the common, and wind up with vingt-un and a glass of grog; the rest come down by the first train to breakfast, when we fill the large room, and have what Ned calls a superb meal; after which we sally forth en masse, and walk across country to the Downs; walk about the course; see the races and all the fun; walk home again; a heavy tea; more vingt-un; and back to town and 'busy life again' the next morning. That's the way to do it. Reader, try it: we shall be happy to see you next year, if there's room. But everything has its drawback, and 'The Bear' is no exception. The Bear himself – I mean the landlord – is a remarkably obtuse, obstinate, and obsolete animal; yet withal obliging enough in his way; a man of few words, and those curt ones; who, as far as my observation extends, never goes out of ear-shot of his premises, and always has a spud in his hand – I believe he goes to bed with it. His wife is likewise of an austere and say-nothing-to-me temperament; but, worst of all, is a bustling little body – a sort of upper house-keeper – who was always telling me I mustn't do this or that, and mustn't do t'other. She has also peculiar notions as to the hours of a gentleman's retiring for the night, and I don't believe any consideration would induce her to let any one in after a quarter past ten. I well remember one night, when, having been spending the evening with a friend, who was lodging in the village, I didn't return till nigh upon twelve: after knocking at the door for a quarter of an hour, the chain was let down, and the little woman, in dressing-gown and curl papers, and a tremendous rage, backed up by an ancient maid (there's no 'girls' there, not they), with a diminutive remnant of candle, was down upon me directly.

'Oh! you bad man; where have you been? You've frighten'd us to death; we've sent for you three times; we've never had such a lodger, and we'll never have you again! Hot water! No, you can't have any hot water; the fire's been out long ago; and that's all the candle you'll have – and mind you put it outside the door before you get into bed; we shall be having the house burnt down, or something. No! I won't say good night – be off with you!'

But she 'means well,' and as I never lose my temper, it's all serene again before long.

M.C. Turner, A Saunter through Surrey (1857). 'The Bear' is still very much with us, although hardly as prettily, as it looks out over a constant stream of traffic. However, the raven deserted Surrey many years ago. Vingt-un is the card game, pontoon.

7 · JOURNEYS

Coaching Days

In 1801 two pair-horse coaches ran between London and Brighton on alternate days – one up, the other down – and they were driven by Crosweller and Hine. The progress of these coaches was an amusing one. The one from London left the 'Blossoms' Inn, Lawrence Lane, at seven a.m., the passengers breaking their fast at the 'Cock', at Sutton, at nine. The next stoppage for the purpose of refreshment was at the 'Tangier' (Banstead Downs), a rural spot, famous for its elderberry wine, which used to be brought from the cottage 'roking hot', and on a cold wintry morning few refused to partake of it. George IV invariable stopped here, and took a glass from the hand of Miss Jeal as he sat in his carriage. The important business of luncheon took place at Reigate, where sufficient time was allowed the passengers to view the Barons' Cave.

William Blew, Brighton and its Coaches *(1894).*

The 'Tally-ho'

'Every week-day of this spring-time the 'Tally-ho' leaves the 'Mitre,' at Hampton Court, for Dorking. At eleven o'clock everything is in readiness save the driver, who puts in a staid and majestic appearance on the box only at the last moment. All around are ostlers and stablemen and men who, although they have nothing whatever to do with the coach, and do not even intend to go by it, are yet drawn here to admire the horses and to surreptitiously pat them after the manner of all Englishmen, who, even if they know nought of the noble animal's 'points,' at least love to see good horse-flesh. Vigorous blasts from 'yards of tin' arouse alarums and excursions, and bring faces to the hotel-windows, reminding one, together with the gold-laced red coat of the guard, of the true coaching age, so eloquently written of by that mighty historian of the road, C.J. Apperley, whom men called 'Nimrod.'

The appointments and the horse-flesh that go to make a first-rate modern turn-out are luxurious beyond anything that 'Nimrod' could have seen, splendid as were some of the crack coaches of his day. Were he here now, he could but acknowledge our superiority in this respect; but we can imagine his critical faculties centred upon what he would have called the 'tooling' of the drag, and his disappointment, not in the workmanship of the driver, but in the excellence of the highways of to-day, which give a coachman no opportunities of showing how resourceful he could be with his wrist, nor how scientific with his 'springing' of his team. Let us compassionate the critic whose well-trained faculties are thus wasted!

But it is full time we were off. A final flourish of the horn, and away we go, our coach making for the heart of Surrey.'
Charles G. Harper, The Portsmouth Road *(1895).*

Nicholas Nickleby on the Portsmouth Road

Modern times of road travel, that range from the reign of George IV to the beginning of the Railway Era, are chiefly filled with stories of the Allied Sovereigns, who ate and drank a great deal too much on their way down to Portsmouth to celebrate the Peace of 1814; of the Duke of Wellington, who followed them in a carriage drawn by eight horses, and ate sparingly and drank little; and all sorts of naval and military bigwigs and left-handed descendants of Royalty who held fat offices in army or navy, and lorded it grandly over meaner, but more legitimate, mortals. No literary or artistic annals belong to this time, saving only the well-known scenes in *Nicholas Nickleby*.

It was on the Portsmouth Road that Nicholas Nickleby and Smike met the redoubtable impresario, Mr. Vincent Crummles. Nicholas, it may be remembered, had fallen on evil times. His capital 'did not exceed, by more than a few halfpence, the sum of twenty shillings,' and so he and Smike were compelled to foot it from London.

"'Now listen to me, Smike,' said Nicholas, as they trudged with stout hearts onwards. 'We are bound for Portsmouth.'

Smike nodded his head and smiled, but expressed no other emotion; for whether they had been bound for Portsmouth or Port Royal would have been alike to him, so they had been bound together.

'I don't know much of these matters,' resumed Nicholas; 'but Portsmouth is a seaport town, and if no other employment is to be obtained, I should think we might get on board some ship. I am young and active, and could be useful in many ways. So could you,' . . .

'Do we go all the way to-day?' asked Smike, after a short silence.

'That would be too severe a trial, even for your willing legs,' said Nicholas, with a good-humoured smile. 'No. Godalming is some thirty and odd miles from London – as I found from a map I borrowed – and I purpose to rest there. We must push on again to-morrow, for we are not rich enough to loiter.'. . .

To Godalming they came at last, and here they bargained for two humble beds, and slept soundly. In the morning they were astir: though not quite so early as the sun: and again afoot; if not with all the freshness of yesterday, still, with enough hope and spirit to bear them cheerily on.

It was a harder day's journey than that they had already performed, for there were long and weary hills to climb; and in journeys, as in life, it is a great deal easier to go down hill than up. However, they kept on, with unabated perseverance, and the hill has not yet lifted its face to heaven that perseverance will not gain the summit of at last.

They walked upon the rim of the Devil's Punch Bowl; and Smike listened with greedy interest as Nicholas read the inscriptions upon the stone which, reared upon that wild spot, tells of a foul and treacherous murder committed there by night. The grass on which they stood had once been dyed with gore; and the blood of the murdered man had run down, drop by drop, into the hollow which gives the place its name. 'The Devil's Bowl,' thought Nicholas, as he looked into the void, 'never held fitter liquor that that!' "

Charles Dickens, reported in Charles G.Harper, The Portsmouth Road *(1895).*
Even Dickens could not resist a mention of the infamous murder of an
unknown sailor in 1786.

Excursion to Portsmouth

On Monday the Reigate and Redhill Band of Hope Union took their annual excursion. This year Portsmouth was the place selected, and, judging from the number who availed themselves of the trip, it was quite as popular as any hitherto organised. The time fixed for starting from Redhill Junction was 8 a.m., and soon after that hour two trains, carrying between them about 1,300 folk of both sexes, and of all sizes, left the station. The morning did not break with large promise of brightness; still so strong was the faith in the day turning out fine that over 70 tickets were sold on the morning of the excursion at the increased price placed on them. A few faint-hearted ones hung back, and great must have been their chagrin as the day advanced, for a more charming day it would have been impossible to select. The trains arrived at Portsmouth at about half-past ten, within a quarter of an hour of each other, and the pleasure-seekers had all their work before them to cram as much into the day as possible, for the trains were timed to return at 7 p.m . . .

In the afternoon steam launches left the Pontoon, Portsmouth Harbour, for Porchester Castle, an ancient fortress about six miles up the Harbour, passing several ironclads, gunnery ships, and Royal yachts, and on the return journey rounding the forts and fleet at Spithead. A little misunderstanding on the part of those managing this trip, which caused a delay of an hour or two in starting, prevented it so being patronised extensively as it otherwise would have been. Time was precious, and the excursionists did not relish the thought of wasting any in waiting, and so drifted off in other directions. Those who went, however, were thoroughly pleased with the sail and view. Lovers of music had the rare treat of listening to the military band, which poured forth sweet strains to a delighted crowd on Southsea Pier from four o'clock to six. There were some few, evidently not members of the Band of Hope, who cared for none of these things, and whose idea of enjoyment was not by any means an elevating one – rather the reverse; and for such Portsmouth, it was quite clear, had afforded abundant gratification, for long before the time arrived for returning, they evinced a decided tendency to go on all fours.

The trains returned to Redhill about 10 p.m., and everyone appeared thoroughly to have enjoyed himself. A few we heard of, whose bump of locality not being very largely developed, and who failed to take the precaution of getting themselves labelled at Portsmouth for the return journey, went wrong. Unfortunately for them, there were other excursions to Portsmouth on Monday from localities widely apart from Redhill. Getting mixed up with these, they took a more circuitous route, and arrived home only in time to be admitted with the milk in the morning.

Surrey Mirror *(August 1879)*. *Well, if things go wrong it's always best to put on a brave face!*

The Motoring Age Begins

'Motoring was very different from today. Journeys took much longer, and if you drove above 40 miles an hour that was considered quite something! My father had a car (a Scripps 'Booth') and would take the family out. The car had no top and when it rained he had to stop and pull the hood over, which had perspex windows in the sides which always seemed to have holes in them. The spare wheel was on the side as well as the petrol can. There were very few garages, so it was wise to always carry petrol. The car often had a puncture. I remember helping my father to mend the puncture and change the wheel. Sometimes an AA man would appear on his bicycle and stop and help you – if you were a member. Going up the hills was always an adventure, and there are plenty of hills in Surrey. The car would easily stall and you had to get out and put stones behind the wheels, and hope you were able to do a hill start without slipping back.'

'In 1920 my father bought his first car – an Austin 20 Tourer. It was obvious that we should have an Austin because both my parents came from Birmingham, where Austins were made. An uncle bought the car for us and drove it down one Saturday. He took father 'round the block' several times on Saturday and again on Sunday morning, but then he had to return home by train and father was on his own! There was no driving test, but of course there were not many cars. After a few weeks we set out for a holiday in Pembrokeshire. It took us two days and several punctures.

The car being a tourer was an open one, but it rained then just as often as it does today. The car was therefore fitted with a hood, which

the manufacturers claimed would unfold from behind the back seats
at the touch of a button and shoot over the passengers so that it could
be fixed to the windscreen and no one got wet. This was the theory,
but in practice we often got drenched.'

Surrey Federation of Women's Institutes, Surrey within Living Memory *(1992).*
I'm not so sure about journeys taking much longer in the 1920s!

Love in a Valley

Take me, Lieutenant, to that Surrey homestead!
    Red comes the winter and your rakish car,
Red among the hawthorns, redder than the hawberries
    And trails of old man's nuisance, and noisier far.
Far, far below me roll the Coulsdon woodlands,
    White down the valley curves the living rail,
Tall, tall, above me, olive spike the pinewoods,
    Olive against blue-black, moving in the gale.

Deep down the drive go the cushioned rhododendrons,
    Deep down, sand deep, drives the heather root,
Deep the spliced timber barked around the summer-house,
    Light lies the tennis-court, plantain underfoot.
What a winter welcome to what a Surrey homestead!
    Oh! the metal lantern and white enamelled door!
Oh! the spread of orange from the gas-fire on the carpet!
    Oh! the tiny patter, sandalled footsteps on the floor!

Fling wide the curtains!—that's a Surrey sunset
    Low down the line sings the Addiscombe train,
Leaded are the windows lozenging the crimson,
    Drained dark the pines in resin-scented rain.
Portable Lieutenant! they carry you to China
    And me to lonely shopping in a brilliant arcade;
Firm hand, fond hand, switch the giddy engine!
    So for us a last time is bright light made.

John Betjeman, Collected Poems *(1966).*

Godstone Station

From Tandridge to Godstone Station it is a long, roundabout, tedious road, which may be shortened here and there by a cut across fields, but in the main has to be taken at its best and worst. There is one old cottage or small farm on the road, and a muddy wood to cross – but Godstone Station is at least two miles and a half from Tandridge. It is about the same distance from everywhere else – a ridiculous station, put down in the middle of a country road, bearing a name to which it has no right whatever, and serving simply as a trap to catch unwary travellers. Here I was doomed to wait three hours for the next train, hungry, cold, tired. I tried the inn near the station – it was a cheerless hole, full of tramps. The evening was closing in; the mists and fog were coming on heavily; the tramps were drunk. I should not like to spend those three hours at Godstone Station over again.

Louis J. Jennings, Field Paths and Green Lanes, *4th edition (1884).*

8 · A HOME IN THE COUNTRY

The spread of London's suburbs into the northern part of Surrey had begun even in the eighteenth century. But it was the building of the railways through the county from 1838 onwards that started the seemingly relentless march of 'suburbia'. Fortunately, this march was halted by the barrier of the North Downs, the interruption of the Second World War and the post-war creation of the 'green belt'.

West Surrey

When I was a child all this tract of country was undiscovered; now, alas! it is overrun.

It is impossible to grudge others the enjoyment of its delights, and yet one cannot but regret, that the fact of its being now thickly populated and much built over, has necessarily robbed it of its older charms of peace and retirement.

Formerly, within a mile or two of one's home, it was a rare thing to see a stranger, and people's lives went leisurely. Now, the strain and throng and unceasing restlessness that have been induced by all kinds of competition, and by ease of communication, have invaded this quiet corner of the land. In the older days, London might have been at a distance of two hundred miles. Now one never can forget that it is at little more than an hour's journey.

Gertrude Jekyll, Old West Surrey (1904).

Smitham Bottom

The hamlet of Smitham Bottom, which paradoxically stands at the top of the pass of that name, in this ancient way across the North Downs, can never have been beautiful. It was lonely when Jackson and Fewterel fought their prize-fight here, before that distinguished patron of sport the Prince of Wales and a more or less distinguished company, on June 9th, 1788; when the only edifice of 'Smith-in-the-Bottom,' as the sporting accounts of that time style it, appears to have been the ominous one of a gibbet. The Jackson who that day fought, and won, his first battle in the prize-ring was none other that that Bayard of the noble art, 'Gentleman Jackson,' afterwards the friend of Byron and of the Prince Regent himself, and subsequently landlord of the 'Cock' at Sutton. On this occasion Major Hanger rewarded the victor with a bank-note from the enthusiastic Prince.

Until 1898 Smitham Bottom remained a fortuitous concourse of some twenty mean houses on a wind-swept natural platform, ghastly with the chalky 'spoil-banks' thrown up when the South Eastern Railway engineers excavated the great cuttings in 1840; but when the three railway-stations within one mile were established that serve Smitham Bottom—the stations of Coulsdon, Stoat's Nest, and Smitham—the place, very naturally, began to grow with the magic quickness generally associated with Jonah's Gourd and Jack's Beanstalk, and now Smitham Bottom is a town. Most of the spoil-banks are gone, and those that remain are planted with quick-growing poplars; so that, if they can survive the hungry soil, there will presently be a leafy screen to the ugly railway sidings. Showy shops, all plate-glass and nightly glare of illumination, have arisen; the old 'Red Lion' inn has got a new and very saucy front; and, altogether, 'Smitham' has arrived. The second half of the name is now in the process of being forgotten, and the only wonder is that the first part has not been changed into 'Smytheham' at the very least, or that an entirely new name, something in the way of 'ville' or 'park,' suited to its prospects, has not been coined. For Smitham, one can clearly see, has a Future, with a capital F, and the historian confidently expects to see the incorporation of Smitham, with Mayor, Town Council, and Town Hall, all complete.

Charles G. Harper, The Brighton Road *(1906).*

Surbiton

Adjoining Kingston is Surbiton, a name which automatically suggests all that is derogatory in the word suburbia. 'Sunday morning in Surbiton' – the phrase makes the heart sink; we can hear the radios playing and smell the Sunday joints roasting in street after painfully genteel street of desirable detached residences; we can see the woman in the fur coat taking her tartan-collared Cairn for a purposive airing under the veiled surveillance of innumerable coyly curtained windows. But why should the name Surbiton be singled out for such associations, for in what respect does it differ from any other of London's dormitories? I cannot answer for I have never visited its streets, but having seen it from the water I would say that it has been maligned. Its riverside walk, bright with beds of flowers, looked pleasant enough, while its riverside houses compare favourably with the bungalows of later date which line other reaches of the Thames – at neighbouring Thames Ditton, for instance, of whose waterfront I carried away an impression only of bungalows and waterworks.

L.T.C. Rolt, The Thames from Mouth to Source *(1951)*.

Destruction of the Countryside

Gordon Home was a keen observer of the Surrey countryside and its towns and villages, and he wrote and illustrated many books about the county over a period of fifty years. Here he bemoans the insensitive destruction of the countryside and also gives us a foretaste of the county's particular problem of today, the motor-car.

Taking a train to some central point from one of the multiplicity of termini used by the great railway which serves the county, we look anxiously from the windows, only to witness on either side the devastating march of the builder who cares naught for delectable landscapes, even if they are among the most superlatively lovely that England – or, indeed, the whole world – has ever produced. A broad and gently rising meadow with an elm-bordered stream at its foot and a belt of pleasant woodland crowning its skyline, which has 'time-out-of-mind' created a sensation of satisfying beauty in all possessed of the power to see with understanding, is in the process of 'development.'

Many of the elms lie prostrate; great drain-pipes suggest that the brook is to be driven from sight, its music to be heard in future by none but rodents; two or three roadways, stark and straight, cut up the swelling curve of the meadow into crude parallelograms, and in them are rising the walls of jaunty little suburban houses. Some are roofed with thin slates brought from Wales, others are covered with V-shaped slabs of composition of an indeterminate reddish hue, some are in pairs, and all have little sheds built alongside them in which to house some form of motor vehicle, for this meadow is near no station, village or township. Those who come to dwell there must be prepared to traverse a mile or two of open country under a like sentence of death at the hands of the builder, and to do this in the twentieth century it seems decreed that one must be provided with some form of locomotion in addition to feet. On this account, between certain hours of the morning, and again in the evening, this newly made patch of outermost London resounds with a great variety of staccato noises. The machine-gun reports of motor-cycles echo among the scarcely dry walls of the villas, and less painful but very noisy vibrations herald the backing-out from tiny garages of a variety of low-powered cars. During week-ends the meadow that we knew a few years ago as silent, save for the infrequent pasing of trains and where cows munched the rich grass, frequently becomes a little battle-field of sounds, many of them deafening. But the inhabitants are mainly youngish people, and none of them cares very much . . .

Gordon Home, The Charm of Surrey *(1929).*

Merridale

Merridale is one of those corners of Surrey where the inhabitants wage a relentless battle against the stigma of suburbia. Trees, fertilized and cajoled into being in every front garden, half obscure the poky 'character dwellings' which crouch behind them. The rusticity of the environment is enhanced by the wooden owls that keep guard over the names of the houses, and by crumbling dwarfs indefatigably poised over goldfish ponds. The inhabitants of Merridale Lane do not paint their dwarfs, suspecting this to be a suburban vice, nor, for the same reason, do they varnish their owls; but wait patiently for the years to endow these treasures with an appearance of weathered antiquity, until one day even the beams in the garage may boast of beetle and woodworm.

John Le Carré, Call for the Dead (1975). There are, perhaps, a number of places in the county which might have served as the author's model!

Surrey Footpaths

From hence the footpath, leaving the copse, descends into a hollow, with a streamlet flowing through a little meadow, barely an acre, with a pollard oak in the centre, the rising ground on two sides shutting out all but the sky, and on the third another wood. Such a dreamy hollow might be painted for a glade in the Forest of Arden . . . A few steps farther and the stile opens on a road.

There the teams travel with rows of brazen spangles down their necks, some with a wheatsheaf for design, some a swan. The road itself, if you follow it, dips into a valley where the horses must splash through the water of a brook spread out some fifteen or twenty yards wide; for, after the primitive Surrey fashion, there is no bridge for waggons. A narrow wooden structure bears foot-passengers; you cannot but linger half across and look down into its clear stream. Up the current where it issues from the fields and falls over a slight obstacle the sunlight plays and glances.

A great hawthorn bush grows on the bank; in spring, white with May; in autumn, red with haws or peggles. To the shallow shore of the brook, where it washes the flints and moistens the dust, the house-martins come for mortar. A constant succession of birds arrive all day long to drink at the clear stream, often alighting on the fragments of chalk and flint which stand in the water, and are to them as rocks.

Another footpath leads from the road across meadows to where the brook is spanned by the strangest bridge, built of brick, with one arch, but only just wide enough for a single person to walk, and with parapets only four or five inches high. It is thrown aslant the stream, and not straight across it, and has a long brick approach. It is not unlike – on a small scale – the bridges seen in views of Eastern travel. Another path leads to a hamlet, consisting of a church, a farmhouse, and three or four cottages – a veritable hamlet in every sense of the word.

In a village a few miles distant, as you walk between cherry and pear orchards, you pass a little shop – the sweets, the twine, and trifles are such as may be seen in similar windows a hundred miles distant. There is the very wooden measure for nuts, which has been used time out of mind, in the distant country. Out again onto the road as the sun sinks, and westwards the wind lifts a cloud of dust, which is lit up and made rosy by the rays passing through it. For such is the beauty of the sunlight that it can impart a glory even to dust.

Once more, never go by a stile (that does not look private) without getting over it and following the path. But they all end in one place. After rambling across furze and heath, or through dark fir woods; after lingering in the meadows among the buttercups, or by the copses where the pheasants crow; after gathering June roses, or, in later days, staining the lips with blackberries or cracking nuts, by-and-by the path brings you in sight of a railway station. And the railway station, through some process of mind, presently compels you to go up on the platform, and after a little puffing and revolution of wheels you emerge at Charing Cross, or London Bridge, or Waterloo, Ludgate Hill, and, with the freshness of the meadows still clinging to you coat, mingle with the crowd.

If it were far away in the distant country you might sit down in the shadow upon the hay and fall asleep, or dream awake hour after hour. There would be no inclination to move. But if you sat down on the sward under the ancient pollard oak in the little mead with the brook, and the wood of which I spoke just now as like a glade in the enchanted Forest of Arden, this would not be possible. It is the proximity of the immense City which induces a mental, a nerve-restlessness. As you sit and would dream a something plucks at the mind with constant reminder; you cannot dream for long, you must up and away, and, turn in which direction you please, ultimately it will lead you to London.

Richard Jefferies, Nature near London *(1883). The author lived at Tolworth and the brook referred to is the Hogsmill. Whilst the nearby railway suburb of Surbiton was already rapidly expanding, a mile or two down the road Jefferies still found abundant wildlife. Twentieth century housing estates were to destroy a great deal of what he observed. However, the little bridge still survives at Ewell.*

Notice to Quit

Here George Sturt illustrates well how the spread of London suburbs and the influx of 'new-comers' brought in by the railways affected every corner of the county. He writes of his own experiences based on the village where he lived, The Bourne near Farnham.

It might be thought that at least when they are at home the people would be untroubled; yet that is not the case. Influences from the new civilization reach them in their cottages, and the intrusion is but the more searching for being impersonal.

It is borne in upon the senses in the shape of sights and sounds proclaiming across the valley that the village is an altered place, that the modern world is submerging it, that the old comfortable seclusion is gone. Even the obscurity of winter nights does not veil the truth; for where, but a few years ago, the quiet depths of darkness were but emphasized by a few glimmering cottage lights, there is now a more brilliant sparkling of lit-up villa windows, while northwards the sky has a dull glare from new road-lamps which line the ridge on its town side. As for the daytime, the labourer can hardly look from his door without seeing up or down the valley some sign or other telling of the invasion of a new people, unsympathetic to his order. He sees, and hears too. As he sweats at his gardening, the sounds of piano-playing come to him, or of the affected excitement of a tennis-party; or the braying of a motor-car informs him that the rich who are his masters are on the road. And though the man should go into his cottage and shut the door, these things must often have for him a sinister meaning which he cannot so easily shut out. There is a vague menace in them. They betoken to all the labouring people that their old home is no longer quite at their disposal, but is at the mercy of a new class who would willingly see their departure.

Perhaps the majority do not feel themselves personally threatened; nevertheless, the situation is disquieting for all. Before the property-owners came, and while still the population was homogeneous, a sort of continuity in the life of the valley impressed itself upon one's consciousness, giving a sense of security. Here amidst the heaths a laborious and frugal people, wise in their own fashion, had their home and supplied their own wants. Not one of them probably thought of the significance of it all, or understood how the village traditions were his inheritance; not one considered what it meant to him to belong to the little group of folk and be independent of the whims of strangers. Yet, for all that, there was a comfort in the situation. To be so familiar as the people were with the peculiarities of the valley, to appreciate the usefulness of the wide heath-land, to value the weather, to comprehend at a glance the doings of the neighbours, and to have fellow-feeling with their motives and hopes and disappointments, was to be at home most intimately, most safely. But all this is a thing of the past. To-day, when the labourer looks around, much of what he sees in the new houses, roads, fences, and so on, has, indeed, been produced by his own handiwork, but it is a product in the enjoyment of which he has no share. It has nothing to do with him and his people; on the contrary, it announces the break-up of the traditional industries by which he lived, and the disintegration of the society of which he was a member. It follows that a certain suggestiveness which used to dignify the home pursuits of the village is wanting to them now. Instead of being a part of the general thrift of the valley – a not unworthy contribution to that which, in the sum, was all important to the village life – those little jobs which the labourer does at home, including his garden-work, have no relation now to anything save his private necessities, because now the dominant interests of the valley are those of a different sort of people who care nothing for such homely things. I shall be told that, after all, this is mere sentiment. But, then, half the comfort of life proceeds from those large vague sentiments which life a man's private doings up from meanness into worthiness. No such enrichment, however – no dim sense of sharing in a prosperous and approved existence – can reward the labourer's industry in this place at the present time. The clever work which, in the village of his equals, would have made him conspicuous and respected, now stamps him as belonging to the least important and least considered section of the population.

Still, I will waive this point. Assuming – though it is much to assume – that the cottagers have no sentiment in the matter, there are other circumstances in the change which cannot fail to disquiet them. I hinted just now that the 'residential' people would not grieve if the labouring folk took their departure. Now, this is no figure of speech. Although it is likely that not one cottager in twenty has any real cause to fear removal, there has been enough disturbance of the old families to prove that nobody is quite safe. Thus, about two years ago, when some cottage property near to a new 'residence' was bought up by the owner of the residence, it was commonly said that he had bought it in order to get rid of some of the tenants, whom he disliked for neighbours. Whether or not that was the real reason I do not know; but certain it is that two of the tenants were forthwith turned out – one of them after twenty-five years of occupancy. It was not the first case of the kind in the village, nor yet the last. At the present moment I know of three families who are likely ere long to have to quit. They live in a block of cottages just beyond the hedge of a substantial house – a block which, it must be owned, is rather an eyesore from there, but which might easily be turned into a decent villa and is actually up for sale for that purpose. And the dwellers in the substantial house are fervently hoping that a buyer of the cottages will soon come forward. They have told me so themselves. 'Of course,' they say, 'we shall be sorry for the poor people to be turned out, but we should like to have nicer neighbours, of our own sort.' So in their own valley these English people are not safe from molestation. With scarce more care for them than would be shown by a foreign invader, gentility pursues its ungentle aims. No cottager can feel quite secure. A dim uncertainty haunts the village, with noticeable effect upon everybody's activities. For a sort of calculating prudence is begotten of it, which is yet not thrift. It dissuades the people from working for a distant future. It cuts off hope, benumbs the tastes, paralyses the aspiration to beautify the home which may any day have to be abandoned.

George Bourne [George Sturt], Change in the Village *(1912)*.

IO · ALL PEOPLE GREAT AND SMALL

A Surrey Archbishop

Aubrey says that the great benefactor of Guildford, Archbishop Abbot, was born in a house now (1692) a public house known by the sign of the Three Mariners, and tells a story that, just previous to his birth his mother dreamt that if she should eat jack or pike her son would be a great man. She was, therefore, very anxious to satisfy her longing and accordingly taking up some of the river water (that ran close by her house) in a pail she caught the fish, dressed it, and devoured it almost all. This story made so much noise that several people of quality offered themselves as sponsors at his baptism, and afterwards maintained him at school and the university.'

The Surrey Magazine, *July 1903. George Abbot was Archbishop of Canterbury from 1611 to 1633.*

Captain Edward Gibbon

This piece about the famous historian was written by E.M. Forster at his house in Abinger.

The garden where I am writing slopes down to a field, the field to a road, and along that road exactly a hundred and seventy years ago passed a young officer with rather a large head. If he had turned the head to the right, he would have seen not me, not the garden, but he would have seen the elms that still border the garden – they were already recognizable trees. And on his left, outrunning him as it has outlived him, ran a little stream called the Tillingbourne. The gorse and the may were just over when he passed, the dog-roses coming out, the bracken rising, but although he was unusually observant he has left no record of these events. 'June was absolutely lost' is his only comment; June, which he might have spent reading Strabo, he was condemned to spend marching across Kent, Surrey and Hants.

He does, however, mention that the previous night he slept at Dorking, and visited there 'a whimsical pretty place in the style of Vauxhall.' I am glad that he should have that relaxation. The pretty place was Denbighs, on the slope of the downs. It was not merely in the style of the Vauxhall garden. It actually belonged to the proprieter, an ingenious gentleman who contrived at every turn some 'singularity,' something that amused and amazed, and the last turn was the most marvelous of all, for it was none other than the Valley of the Shadow of Death itself. A guide book of the period thus describes the scene:

'The view on the descent into this gloomy vale was awful. There was a large alcove, divided into two compartments, in one of which the Unbeliever was represented dying in great agony. Near him were his books which encouraged him in his libertine course, such as Hobbes, Tindal, etc. In the other was the good Christian, calm and serene, taking a solemn leave of the World, and anticipating the joys of immortality.'

The young officer must have regarded the alcove with an easy and an equal smile. He was rather conceited and he may have foreseen that before long, in the libertine's library, a work of his own would be lying, a work more suggestive than even Tindal and Hobbes, and entitled *The Decline and Fall of the Roman Empire*.

Yes; it was Edward Gibbon who passed at the bottom of this garden on June 8th, 1761. He strikes me as a little dissatisfied. He is fresh from a wretched love-affair; he wanted to marry a Swiss girl, and his father objected. 'I sighed as a lover, I obeyed as a son,' he will write in after years, but the episode is not yet an epigram. He is vaguely unhappy, and his father has married again – depressing. Then there is money – he needs it for books and dissipation, and has consented to cutting off an entail in return for £300 a year – a bad bargain. Then there is religion – it is all very well to smile at the alcove, but one must belong somewhere, and he has already changed from Protestantism to Catholicism and back again; the Swiss girl was a protestant. And then – overshadowing everything – is a vexatious war. England is at war with France. Our ally, Prussia, is beating France, yet we are afraid of a French invasion, and a militia Bill has been passed authorizing the raising of troops for home defence. It seemed an excellent measure, and he and his father were both enthusiastic. Alas! Their services have been accepted, and here they are, a captain and a major in the South Hampshire Militia, and they are making constant route marches, drilling, recruiting, guarding dirty prisoners, entertaining people whom they do not want to meet, quarrelling with people whom they have never seen, and engaged in a war otherwise unknown to history – the war between the South Hampshire Militia and the North. The major is bored – still, he wastes his life wherever he is, and we need not pity him. The captain wants to read, study, think, but this aggravating little trap has caught him. Nor is he feeling physically well – the grotesque disease which will finally carry him off has already declared itself. However, this he mentions to no one, any more than he mentions the love-affair, and his outward deportment is frigid and bland. Westward he goes, and, looked at through all those years and those myriads of fallen leaves, he seems romantic to me – the greatest historian England has ever produced, trying his paces on the English roads. But he found no romance in them himself, no anywhere until he heard vespers in the church of Ara Coeli. His head – moving away from mine by now – is not yet concentrated on the decline and fall. Other schemes contend inside it, such as the life of Sir Walter Raleigh, or a history of that noble people, the Swiss, or a monograph of the talented Medici at Florence. And his little book about literature has just come out written in French, and he will present a copy to the Duke of York if opportunity offers. Nursing his secrets, he disappears in the direction of Guildford and I lose him as a neighbour. It is surprising he ever came so near.

E.M.Forster, Abinger Harvest (1936).

Miss Gertrude Jekyll

The following was written shortly before Surrey's most famous gardener, Gertrude Jekyll, published her first book, Wood and Garden, *in 1899.*

December 10th – There has been in this year's 'Guardian' a succession of monthly papers on a Surrey garden, written by Miss Jekyll of Munstead Wood, Godalming. I give her address as she now sells her surplus plants, all more or less suited to light soils, to the management of which she has for many years past given special attention. These papers have much illuminating matter in them, and are called 'Notes from Garden and Woodland.' All the plants and flowers about which Miss Jekyll writes she actually grows on the top of her Surrey hill. Her garden is a most instructive one, and encouraging too. She has gone through the stage, so common to all ambitious and enthusiastic amateurs, of trying to grow everything, and of often wasting much precious room in growing inferior plants, or plants which, even though they may be worth growing in themselves, are yet not worth the care and feeding which a light soil necessitates if they are to be successful.

This, to me, rather delightful characteristic of amateurs in every art was severely condemned by Mr Ruskin in my youth, when he said that the amateur sketcher always attempted to draw the panorama of Rome on his thumb-nail, instead of humbly trying to reproduce what was at his own door. The practice is just as common in gardening as in music and painting.

Every plant that Miss Jekyll names is worth getting and growing in gardens that are of considerable size, and which more or less share her Surrey soil and climate. I trust that before long these articles will be republished in book form, for every word in them deserves attention and consideration.

Mrs C. W. Earle, Pot-Pourri from a Surrey Garden *(1897).*

The Duke of York's Birthday Celebrations at Oatlands, Weybridge

A grand fête was given at Oatlands on Monday, by the Duchess of York, in honour of the Duke's birthday; and was one of the most cheerful of the season, equally gladdening the hearts of the Prince and peasant. The dinner, of twenty-four courses, was one of the best and most elegant that ever came up to table. Among the company were, the Prince of Wales, Duke of Clarence, Lady Ann Smith, Sir John Shelly, Mr. Fawkener, Mrs Greenwood, a German Baron, the Gentlemen of the Household, and some of the neighbouring Gentlemen; amongst whom were Mr. Pippin, the High Sheriff of the County, Mr. Robson, and Mr. Page. In the evening the pleasure-ground was illuminated, and the skittle-ground was prepared for the domestics and neighbours to dance, which they did till six o'clock in the morning. The Duchess, Lady Ann, and the Prince, all danced; Prince, Princess, and stable-boys and house-maids altogether, in the true style of jubilee domestic merry-making. For the dinner company an elegant supper was prepared at the Grotto: the grounds around it were lighted up. The Duke's Band played the whole time. The Prince and Duchess, &c. &c. sang Catches and Glees; and kept up the spirit of the entertainment till near seven in the morning. There was a supper in a large house of a tenant for the friends of the Upper Servants. The whole evening's entertainment never was surpassed for conviviality and hospitality.

Morning Chronicle, *1802*.

The Founding of Georgia

James Oglethorpe was the driving force behind the establishment of the Colony of Georgia, now the State in the U.S.A.. His country seat was at Westbrook, Godalming.

The *Ann Galley*, of above 200 Tons, is on the point of sailing from Deptford, for the new Colony of Georgia, with 35 Families, consisting of Carpenters, Bricklayers, Farmers, &c. who take all proper Instruments. The Men are learning Military Discipline of the Guards, as must all that go thither, and carry Musquets, Bayonets, and Swords, to defend the Colony in case of an Attack from the Indians. She has on board 10 Ton of Alderman Parson's best Beer, and will take in at the Maderas 5 Tun of Wine, for the Service of the Colony. James Oglethorpe, Esq; one of the Trustees, goes with them to see them settled.

Annual Register, *Monday 30 October, 1732*.

Lord Onslow

Lord Onslow lives near Merrow. This is the man that was, for many years, so famous as a driver of four-in-hand. He used to be called Tommy Onslow. He has the character of being a very good landlord. I know he called me 'a d—d Jacobin' several years ago, only, I presume, because I was labouring to preserve to him the means of still driving four-in-hand, while he, and others like him, and their yeomanry cavalry, were working as hard to defeat my wishes and endeavours. They say here, that, some little time back, his Lordship, who has, at any rate, had the courage to retrench in all sorts of ways, was at Guildford in a gig with one horse, at the very moment, when Spicer, the Stock-broker, who was a Chairman of the Committee for prosecuting Lord Cochrane, and who lives at Esher, came rattling in with four horses and a couple of out-riders! They relate an observation made by his Lordship, which may, or may not, be true, and which therefore, I shall not repeat. But my Lord, there is another sort of courage; courage other than that of retrenching, that would become you in the present emergency; I mean political courage and especially the courage of acknowledging your errors; confessing that you were wrong when you called the reformers Jacobins and levellers; the courage of now joining them in their efforts to save their country, to regain their freedom, and preserve to you your estate, which is to be preserved, you will observe, by no other means that that of a Reform of the Parliament.

William Cobbett, Rural Rides (1830). Little appears to change in politics!

Old Country Folk

It is sad to think that, within a few years, death will have claimed the few yet living of the old people who retain the speech and manner of the earliest part of the nineteenth century. Born and brought up in remote and quiet country villages and hamlets, many of them can neither read nor write, and I have met with some who have never been ten miles away from their birthplace. But they are by no means among the dull ones of the earth; indeed, their simple wisdom and shrewdness are in many ways quite equal to those of their brethren in the wider world.

Their lives have been perhaps all the happier in that they have been concerned with few wants and few responsibilities; and if their thoughts are mainly of hay-time and harvest, and root-crops, and the care of sheep and cattle, shall we presume to think that these interests are of less account than our own; for, after all, what can be of greater need or of more supreme importance?

They are good to have to do with, these kindly old people. Bright and cheerful of face, pleasant and ready of speech, courteous of manner, they are a precious remnant of those older days when men's lives were simpler and quieter; free from the stress and strain and restless movement, and endless hurry and struggle against time, and from all the petty worrying distractions that fret the daily life of the more modern worker. So pleasantly does this make itself felt that to be with one of these old people for an hour's quiet chat is a distinctly restful and soothing experience.

It is good to hear their ideas of life, and their stories of actual experience, told in the homely wording of their limited vocabulary, and there is a charm in the cheery old country voice, with its whimsical twists of quavering modulation. And no less pleasant is the old country manner, whose ready courtesy expresses kindly welcome and cordial good fellowship.

Among these old folks one hears with pleasure many a terse old phrase and local saying, and many a word of good old English, that those who have the pretension of knowing better have somehow lost, either by sheer neglect, or by letting some rank weed of a word grow up and choke and kill, and usurp the place of one so much older and better. For instance, the fine old verb 'to abide' is still in their mouths.

'Bide still' says the cottage grandmother to a restless child, or 'I'll bide at home till the rain gives over.'

'Stand on a cheer, Gooerge, ye'll have moor might,' said an old father, when his son was trying to pull a nail out of a beam at arm's length. 'Might' in this sense is nearly lost to us; the only hold we seem to keep of it, except in the adjective and adverb forms, is in the idioms, 'with all his might' and 'with might and main.' Why have we become so shy of the good old words? I hear the old carpenter say of the new gate-post, 'Rare (rear) it up,' and of the tree-trunk 'Saw it asunder,' whereas I suppose we should say 'Stand it up on end,' or 'Stand it upright' and 'Saw it in two' or 'Saw it across,' surely all weaker and more cumbersome ways of saying the same thing . . .

There are a number of old local names of birds and small wild animals, &c., some of which are still in use. Thus, the green woodpecker is a 'yaffles,' the wagtail a 'dish-washer'; the wren a 'puggy' or 'juggy-wren'; the nightjar is called 'puckridge' or 'eve-jar'; the swift, 'squeaker'; the whitethroat, 'nettle-creeper' or 'hay-builder'; the red-backed shrike, 'butcher-bird' or 'bee-eater'; the common heron, 'Jack-heron,' and the wryneck, 'rining-bird.' This bird comes at the time when oak-bark is stripped. 'When we hears that we very soon thinks about rining the oaks.' 'Rine' (rind) is the usual equivalent of bark.

The dormouse is called 'sleeper' or 'sleeper-mouse'; the long-tailed field-mouse 'bean-eater'; the field-vole and bank-vole 'sheep-dog mouse.'

The large stag-beetles are 'pincher-bobs,' cock-chafers are 'may-bees,' the large dragon-flies are 'adder-spears.'

The rabbits' burrow is always a 'bury.' Young geese are 'gulls,' never goslings.

'Agen' is an interesting old word. 'Agen the ge-at' (both g's hard) does not mean 'against the gate,' but 'near the gate.' It seems to have the same sense as the 'over against' of the Bible.

Gertrude Jekyll, Old West Surrey (1904). I can add 'cheesy-bob' for a woodlouse, a term which is still used in parts of south-west Surrey. Gertrude Jekyll's rosy view of the life of country people did not always reflect the truth of what was often a hard life of poverty and struggle.

Working in the Jekyll Household

I went into domestic service when I was 14, in 1920. I went to the local vicar in Bramley, the Rev David Green. It was not compulsory but it seemed to be the idea that young girls stayed about a year or 18 months to get a grounding; then they were expected to get a better position with some other household, which of course happened with myself.

After several posts gaining experience I obtained a post with the

Jekylls in Munstead. I worked with them until I got married. That is how I knew Getrude Jekyll, because her brother, Sir Herbert, for whom I worked, had the old house when their mother died and Gertrude built or was building her own house in Munstead Wood. They were on opposite sides of the road so they were in and out of each other's houses all the time.

Gladstone gave the Jekylls a parrot, called Polly. The housekeeper would let it out of the cage and it would go running through the corridors and if the phone rang it shouted at the top of its voice 'Aggie! Aggie! The phone!' 'Aggie' was Lady Jekyll and it was telling her to come to the phone in the servants hall! It rather terrified the younger members of the staff. I once saw it get on the back of a chair behind a visiting chauffeur and nip him, right through the ear. It was rather vicious really, The footman and the groom, who lived in the house, used to get it into the downstairs bathroom and tell it all sorts of things to repeat, so you can imagine what it was like! Sir Herbert had a little dog, Jock, a lovely little Aberdeen. He was terrified of the parrot, of its getting on his back. Oh yes, it was a real horror, but I always got on alright with it—as long as you were very, very careful. When I was at Munstead House, you started at half past six in the morning and you were lucky if you got to bed at ten o'clock at night. If you were lucky you might get an hour in the afternoon to sit down or go shopping. You got out for half a day; they called it an afternoon and evening but sometimes it had got to three o'clock before you got away. You got this once a week, and every other Sunday. You were expected to go to church Sunday morning and then you got the rest of the day. And we had one week's holiday a year, when you usually went home to see your people.

In the beginning I used to get £12 a year, paid only once in three months. Out of that you had to buy your uniforms, so you did not get very much, but you managed. I paid my mother half a crown because she did my personal washing when I wanted her to. That was about once a month. The household laundry used to go the Godalming laundry.

You had a good living if you were with a good household. Munstead House was excellent. Their social life started about Friday until Monday or Tuesday. The house was full of visitors and it was an entertaining time. I was able to meet very interesting people, in the art world in particular. One of the nieces, Margaret Post, was married to Mark Hamburg, the pianist, and I also met ballet dancers. Lydia Lopkokova, wife of John Maynard Keynes, used to come – the idea of inviting such people was that they entertained the other visitors. We had an enclosed yew garden where all the yew trees were carved out and marble figures stood in them, and in the centre was a lilypond, and I saw her dancing there many times at weekends.

In the household we had three staff in the pantry – a butler, a footman and the boot boy. There were three housemaids, three in the kitchen, a chauffeur and a groom outside, plus the gardeners.

I was in the Jekyll household for about two and a half to three years. Then I got married. If I had not, I should have gone with Sir Herbert's sister, Mrs Eden, whose husband had been the planner and maker of the Garden of Eden in Venice.

Surrey Federation of Women's Institutes, Surrey Within Living Memory *(1992).*

The Furze-cutter and the Gypsies

Here is an American's romantic view of life in the countryside of Victorian Surrey.

It always seemed that Merrow would repay one for a long ramble, yet the heath lying to the right became a sort of magnet to us, and we liked to spend quiet hours of reflection or work there. I think we Americans enjoy no bit of English country more than a heath, or moor, or down. There must be some peculiar reason for this aside from the associations of fiction. The Merrow downs are wide and sunny stretches, with a roadway going up and down and zigzag across the downs, and out to an open space, whence you can see all the loveliness of Leith Hill, vales and meadows, church and manor-house, lying below you, but the portion of the heath I learned to care for most was just where the road 'lifted' a little between the furze bushes, and where, when we were first in Surrey, the traditional furze-cutter was at work. It was delightful one morning to come upon a little caravan with smoke rising from it, and a flapping cutain, and to see its owner – a tall figure in corduroys, and a jacket belted in, and long gauntlets – cutting away at the furze. The man used a sort of scythe, and bent and swayed very picturesquely as he worked. The occupation looked a noble sort of one, because, I suppose, it was so useful, and, besides, it was out-of-door employment, which to my mind always has a grand suggestion of ownership of all nature. This furze-cutter was a far more enviable figure than Millet's concentrated dark peasants sowing the earth with dogged persistence. Yet on a windy April moor the man suggested Millet's palette and brush. While we were looking at him across the road-side, he broke out into a rough, light-hearted sort of singing, tuneless rather, but inspiring, and in keeping with the honest sunshine of the morning. The words did not reach us, but there was something about 'up, ye boys – up, ye boys,' in it which I liked to listened to, and which made me feel sure the man was healthy and contented. He had a big sunburned face and a stubby light beard, and when he looked up from his work his eyes had the glance of one new to meeting strong sunlight. nThe furze-cutters were not the only figures on the heath. One day when our party chanced to feel particularly alone, and inclined to lotus-eating, for everywhere there seemed a balm in the pale spring lights about us – we looked up, and crossing a ridge was a strange procession. The figures toiled into prominence one after another, descended, drew nearer, gathering together separate identities, and then resolved themselves into a troop of wandering or travelling gypsies, by far the most picturesque I have ever seen. First came two very swarthy-looking men, all blacks and browns, until they drew nearer, and certain yellow lights spotted them here and there; they were followed by a young woman and two children; then two more women and a youth; the next one, a sorry-looking horse drawing a cart with a curtained top, and when the procession drew nearer, we saw that this contained a young woman with a very tiny black-haired baby, evidently newly born, for the only anxiety of the party seemed to be the well-being of these two. Perhaps the last two figures were the most entertaining. These were a donkey, and an old woman whose nut of a face was tied up in a gay bandana. The donkey proceeded, as donkeys will, with various aggravating little halts and attempts to nibble at the road-side, and as the little procession curved past where we sat, we could hear the old woman talking to it in the most absurdly conversational tone.

'Just *you* wait till we be to Dorking,' she said, in low monotone. '*You'll* see if you can act so.' A pause, during which the donkey became calmly contemplative of the scene to his right – Leith Hill, St. Katherine's, a rich and changing line of meadow-lands, with gray spires in the faint spring foliage. 'What you waitin' for *now*?' the old woman went on. 'Never seen a walley before, I'd suppose.' The donkey slowly moved on. ' Oh, you *are* a beast,' she continued, monotonously, beating him with a short stick – a beast – a beast – a beast.' No opposition being offered to this criticism, she seemed to feel it worth renewing, and as the troop descended the hilly slope toward Dorking, we could hear the thwack of her stick and the same remark, 'A beast – a beast.'

John Lillie, 'In Surrey' (published in Harper's New Monthly Magazine, September 1882).

The Creator of Sherlock Holmes

Arthur Conan Doyle built a house on the heights of Hindhead in the hope that its location would help to improve the health of his first wife, who suffered from TB. Although she died from the disease in 1906, the famous author always maintained that the clean air of 'the English Switzerland' had considerable prolonged her life.

At 'Undershaw' lives Dr. Conan Doyle. His house stands at the corner of the road, on the edge of a hollow, but is almost buried from view by a great tangled mass of wild-growing trees, climbing brambles, and undergrowth. It overlooks a wide valley, where the novelist, with his experience of the South African campaign vividly fresh in mind, has established a shooting range. Straight as the bullet from his rifle, or the ball from his cricket bat, come the words from his pen. All that he writes is simple, natural, and to the point, never prosy or long-winded, first and before all the work of a man and sportsman. He loves a good fighter, yet he can write a tender domestic idyll like 'The Duet.' In his versatility and his wanderings he compares with Grant Allen. He has written poetry, history, plays, novels of various periods and of various climes, detective stories, sea stories, ringing ballads, and for all he has delighted readers. He has sailed the Artic as doctor of a Scotch whaler, broiled on the malarial coast of West Africa, served with a field hospital in South Africa. He has given us Hordle John, Micah Clarke, Sir Nigel Loring, Decimus Saxon, Brigadier Gerard, Rodney Stone,

Cullingworth, the world-famed Sherlock Holmes, and many another creation that lives in the memory and comes unbidden to mind. What days of pleasure he has provided us since, twenty-three years ago, when a medical student in Edinburgh (where he was born in 1859), he first appeared as an author in 'The Mystery of the Sassassa Valley.' How many of the few who read it dreamt he would become one of the most popular authors not only in England, but wherever the English language is spoken? And perhaps the rarest feature of his success is that criticism and the popular voice are in accord. Which is really his best book is a question that may not be decided by his contemporaries. In his genial way he himself assures us that the best thing he ever wrote was 'The Narrative of John Smith.' The manuscript was lost in the post, and has never since been heard of. 'But I must in all honesty confess,' adds its author, 'that my shock at its disappearance would be as nothing to my horror if it were suddenly to appear again – in print.' It is safe to say that there are many who wish for nothing better than 'Micah Clarke' or 'The White Company.'

Duncan Moul & Gibson Thompson, Picturesque Surrey *(1902). Maybe that missing manuscript will drop through my letter box one day! Grant Allen, who was a near neighbour to Conan Doyle, and an equally famous writer at the time, is now almost forgotten.*

Missing Novelist Mystery

What has become of Mrs Christie, the novelist, whose motor-car was found abandoned in a bush on Saturday morning in a lane leading from Newlands Corner to Albury?

Scores of police, augmented by special constables, civilians, and others have been endeavouring to supply the answer to this question during the week, and in their search of the downs and woods at Newlands Corner they have been aided by dogs, aeroplanes, and a tractor.

Up to yesterday afternoon the question remained unanswered, and the Surrey County police admit that the mystery is the most baffling they have had to deal with. Ponds, lakes and streams in the neighbourhood have been searched, dragged and in some cases drained; plantations above and below Newlands Corner have been combed as effectively as the forces available would permit; clues have been followed up and theories examined, but the question remains— where is Mrs Christie?

Mrs Agatha Clarissa Christie, the missing woman, is the wife of Colonel Christie of The Styles, Sunningdale, and is a novelist, a writer chiefly of detective and mystery stories. She is described as being aged 35, 5ft 7ins in height, with reddish hair, shingled, grey eyes, and fair complexion: wearing a grey stockinette skirt, green jumper, grey cardigan, and small velour hat. She had a platinum ring with one pearl, but no wedding ring, and may have had a black handbag containing at the time of her disappearance probably £5 to £10.

On Friday Mrs Christie visited her mother in law, a Mrs Hemsley, at Dorking, and then returned home. At 9.45 p.m. she is stated to have again left home, leaving a note that she was going for a drive, and would not be back that night.

The next morning, at about eight o'clock, her car was found, as stated, resting against the bank of the track leading to Albury, and but a short distance from Newlands Corner. In the car were certain articles of clothing, etc., which belonged to Mrs Christie, but no trace of the woman herself could be found.

Surrey Advertiser, *11th December, 1926. A December evening was a very strange time to choose for a drive, but I will leave it to you to solve the mystery!*

10 · ON THE HUSTINGS

Gatton

Until the Reform Act of 1832 Gatton, with the smallest electorate possible, provided two M.P.s!

According to tradition each representative of this pocket Borough, which Cobbett in his *Rural Rides* designates 'a very rascally spot of earth,' was mulcted in a fee of £1,000 per election. It is not surprising that the owner welcomed dissolutions and that he proved so loyal to his political rights and convictions that he jealously safeguarded the privilege of election; thus, when Whigs and Tories were so evenly divided that the declaration of the Poll disclosed four voting for and three against the owner's nominees, he is said to have disenfranchised all electors but himself by making them weekly tenants, and a record exists of an Indenture dated 1542, preserved in the Rolls Chapel, that Sir Roger Copley, Knt., therein described as 'Burgess and oonly inhabitant of the Borough and Town of Gatton,' freely elected and chose two burgesses for Parliament 'having sure and perfect knowledge of their good discrec'on on larning and wysdome.' As a result of this disenfranchisement Gatton can claim the distinction of being the only Parliamentary constituency in Great Britain where female suffrage has been exercised, Lady Copley by right of tenure having nominated and elected two members of Parliament. Little wonder that such constituencies were designated 'Rotten'! The ancient Town Hall alone remains an interesting link with the past. This quaint little building fronting the entrance gates reminds one very much of a Greek Temple, and its style, although simple, is certainly very beautiful *(see illustration on the previous page)*. It appealed to the artist, Birket Foster, who remarked that he had never before depicted a Town Hall which was given over to the rabbit and squirrel. If only it could speak, what tales it could tell of noble ambitions or thoughtless venture; what local pride and importance it long had marked, and now – well, we should not have estimated it at its true worth any more than the powers who disenfranchised so important a centre as Gatton, whose members claimed to be the only free and independent legislators since they could ignore their constituents' views. As an election curiosity it may be mentioned that the sum total of a contested election was £22 8s., of which £14 12s. represented wines and beer!

T.G.W. *Henslow,* Gatton Park *(1914).*

Haslemere Elections

Only property owners were entitled to vote in parliamentary elections and, as a result, bribery and the artificial division of freeholds to create extra votes occurred frequently. Haslemere was another notorious 'rotten' borough but the Reform Act of 1832 removed this town's right to send two members to the House of Commons.

He [General James Oglethorpe] failed to gain a seat in the election of 1754, which was also memorable for the use made of the Red Cow public-house in Petworth Road. Of this one burgage, which usually provided one vote for the owner, eight votes were manufactured by subdivision of the freehold, and six or seven more from the White Hart and White Horse Inns. . .

At the elections more and more voting power was literally bought by certain candidates, by the means of buying up the local freehold property.

After the celebrated 1754 election there was a House of Commons enquiry at which the late Mr. Webb was accounted to own thirty votes, Mr. Molyneux ten votes, and Mr. Burrell nine votes. Mr. Webb's burgage holdings had cost £20,000 and produced a rental of £160 per annum, but could now be bought for £15,000. . .

In 1776 Sir James Lowther bought the Haslemere Manor and a number of the burgage freeholds, the remainder being bought by the Burrell family, so that by 1791 there were no independent burgage holders, and till the end of the century Lowther and Burrell, or their nominees, were consistently returned.

G.R. Rolston, Haslemere in History *[contained in 'Haslemere'] (1978).*

Haslemere Election Song 1761

. . . Col. Molyneux and Mr. Webb had, in anticipation, made sundry arrangements to share the costs of the next election, and they found themselves opposed by the Burrell and other interests, represented by a Mr. Richard Muilman and Mr. Thomas Parker, of whose history and personal claims to the confidence of the electors there is little information, save that afforded by an unfriendly political squib, in which Mr. Muilman is described as a 'Mynheer from Amboyna,' and Mr. Parker as a 'Tike' and a 'prig from the North.'

Haslemere Contest. 'Tune of Hearts of Oake.'

Ye Haslemere Voters attend to my Song
and learn to distinguish between right and wrong
Your Neybours prefer nor their offors despise
for as ye are Honest so may ye be wise.

Then Vote for no Tike no Dutch Sooterkin
but always be hearty and true to your Party
for Mollyneux and Webb Agen and Agen.

A prig from the North all your Votes does Implore
and fresh from Amboyna Mynheer is come o'er
but free men like us will have no Yorkshire bite
and a Sooterkin Member the Women would fright.

In truth Hogan Mogan away you may steer

and give up your hopes and your Interest here
'tis Freedom we boast, and will stick to our Cause
Shall Dutch Men presume to give Brittons their Laws.

And Parker the Prig you may too take your leave
Adieu to your schemes and your Ark [?Art] to deceive
go Humbug your Masters your cunning pursue
get money from them to buy Boroughs for you.

then to the old Members we'll Push the Glass round
their Hearts they are good & their Principles sound
our rights they maintain, Then who would refuse
such Healths for to Pledge or such Members to Choose.

then we'll Vote for no Tike nor Dutch Sooterkin
but always be Hearty, and true to our Party,
for Mollyneux and Webb, Agin and Agin.

The election took place in March, 1761, and Col. Molyneux and Mr. Webb were returned by 52 votes as against 34 given to their opponents.

E.W. *Swanton*, Bygone Haslemere *(1914)*.

A Guildford Election

The chicanery common to the democratic process in the eighteenth century is further well illustrated by the election for Guildford's two Members of Parliament in 1790. Again, only freeholders of property were entitled to vote and the secret ballot was a long way off. Perhaps elections these days are just a little less open to corruption!

The party disputes at the time of the elections were also a fruitful source of disorder, and it may be interesting perhaps to review the procedure at one of them, as the habits of the time have so completely changed . . .

The precept for the writ was received by the Mayor from Mr. Samuel Long, the Sheriff, and, on the 21st of June, at eight o'clock in the morning, the Mayor, assisted by A. Piggott, his counsel, came to the Town Hall. The Acts for the prevention of bribery and corruption and for preventing others than freemen from voting were read, and the three candidates were proposed.

The Hon. Thomas Onslow was proposed by Mr. John Shrubb and supported by Mr. William Newland, the old doctor then resident where Miss Wenham's school was lately carried on. The Hon. Major-General Chapple Norton was proposed by Mr. Martyr and supported by Mr. Smith, and Mr. George Sumner was nominated by Mr. Skurrey and supported by the Rev. Mr. Clifton.

The poll commenced at ten o'clock and closed at five that same afternoon, and it was an interesting performance, as each candidate was represented by counsel, who had the privilege of questioning the voters one by one as they came to record their votes. All the questions and answers were taken down and afterwards printed, and from the books of the proceedings the information as to these elections is taken. The counsel were empowered to call for the production of the deeds of the property under which freeholders claimed, but in many cases the deeds were not produced, and the voters refused to produce them.

A Mr. William Parsons, scrivener, of High Street, voting for Sumner, was seriously questioned whether, having two houses, one in and one without the town, the former was not expressly retained for the purposes of the vote. He explained that he used it as an office, but did not live there, but he had lodged for forty nights in the house. The rent he paid was £7 a year, and he let off part of it for four guineas, so he had a vote for less than £3 a year. Mr. John Oliver, of High Street, was questioned in the following way:

'How long have you had your freehold?'
'About three weeks.'
'Do you not mean to sell directly after the election?'
'I never mean to sell it.'
'Did you not say how you would vote if that house was not sold?'
'No, I did not.'
'Did not your landlord say that he had sold the house in order that his tenant might vote?'

These words being proved, it was held that a man who takes property on the eve of an election should not be admitted to vote, but the opposing counsel cleverly made out that no one could have known for certain three weeks before the election that an election was to take place, although they might have fancied it would do, and there was, therefore, no legal proof that the property was obtained for the vote, and it was allowed.

Mr. Henry Horner, a carpenter, claimed to vote for a house conveyed to him only the previous day by Mr. Hockley, which, the counsel affirmed, was to be re-conveyed back the day the election was over. Here, again, there could be no legal proof; and, as the first conveyance was in order, the vote was passed.

Mr. Solomon Saker, a patten-maker, declared that he had bought his own premises, but could produce no conveyance. Mr. Dunn, the agent to Lord Cranley, happened, however, most conveniently to be in court, and in reply to a question gave the equivocal answer that Lord Cranley received no rent from Saker now. This was accepted as primâ facie evidence that Lord Cranley had sold and Saker had bought the property, and the vote was allowed.

Another voter had always paid rates up till quite lately, but for two years no rates had been demanded, and he therefore concluded that the property had been given him, and that he was a freeholder, and voted accordingly.

In another case, the rate collector had forgotten to make up his book, and he stated he believed the voter owned the house in which he lived, but was not quite sure. The voter himself declared that he did, but had forgotten when he bought it, and the vote was passed.

Mr. Benjamin Keene was questioned as to whether he or his wife received parochial relief, which would have invalidated his vote, but neither he nor Mrs Keene were able to remember as to whether they ever had received it, and the somewhat curious lapse of memory affected the various witnesses in court, who could none of them be quite sure whether the Keenes had been in receipt of relief or not. Oddly enough, the relief-book could not be found; but, as the Mayor stated that it would take a long time to search for it, and other voters were coming along, he passed the vote.

Mr. Samuel Cole, of the Grammar School, declared that one wall of a stable was his freehold, and proved it from the fact that he put a cow in the stable. Nobody had ever seen the cow in the stable till the previous day, but that did not matter, and Mr. Cole's claim to vote was allowed.

Mr. Vincent said he had a wine-cellar and kept wine in it. Twelve bottles, he declared, were his; the owner of the rest of the bottles, believing that Mr. Vincent was right, stated that these twelve bottles were certainly not his property, therefore Mr. Vincent was declared freeholder of the cellar, and he had his vote. . .

The poll at five o'clock stood as follows: Onslow, 67; Norton, 43; Sumner, 46, the voters having been only 86 in number. Of all these, four, being citizens of London, were not questioned at all, the Mayor stating that, inasmuch as they had come all the way from London to vote, it was quite clear that they possessed votes, and it would only waste the time of the court to ask them what these votes were.

The next day, at ten o'clock, the court opened, but General Norton at once announced that he found there was an apparent majority against him; and, although it was but small – three only – it was yet decisive, and would not permit him to continue the poll. A memorandum in the poll-book shows that he had polled all his votes, whereas his opponents had a few more to come, and he therefore resigned, and Onslow and Sumner were declared elected.

The expenses of the counsel for the Mayor were divided amongst the three candidates . . . The poll-book then records the speeches of the candidates, with the following quaint statement at the end, that 'as it is not expected, so it cannot be the wish of the gentlemen to see the whole of their extemporary orations printed, not to say that it might give cause of offence to them.'

In Mr. Sumner's speech he admitted himself to be overcome with gratitude to the electors, and unable to say more, but he continued speaking for more than half-an-hour longer. There were only two hundred persons qualified to vote at that time, and the Beadle who lived at Rat's Gate, Mr. Peché, the Surveyor of Windows, Mr. Sturt the painter, Mr. Dowlen the collar-maker, and Mr. William Russell the musician, were all voting elsewhere, and several other people declared to their great regret that they were unable to vote for either candidate, or were ill.

As soon as the election was over, the public-houses were thrown open, the two Members paying for whatever was required, and a scene of great disorder ensued, and a riot which extended far into the night.

George C. Williamson, Guildford in the Olden Time *(1904).*

The Borough of Bletchingley

When we turn to Bletchingley, which enjoyed the status of a Parliamentary Borough from 1295 to 1832, we have a record of 216 elections, including 25 intermediate, and 308 Members to share such honour as attached to its representation . . .

'The Right Worshipful Sir Thomas Carwarden, knight,' who was the Member in 1547, fell on troublous times. His residence at Bletchingley Castle was seized and searched, and was found to contain far more than the armour of a few retainers and the artillery of a deer park – enough to arm a hundred horse and more than 300 foot. All were conveyed to the Tower, and Sir Thomas, in his petition and protest, attributed his arrest and seizure of his goods, 'which were conveyed in 17 great waynes thoroughly laden,' to certain most untrue surmises. Queen Mary could prove nothing against him, and he was liberated. He died shortly afterwards at Horsley, and the funeral took place at Bletchingley, where, it is said, the villagers 'mourned with the best beef and beer' at a cost of £149. Sir Thomas Browne, knt, of Betchworth, won the seat in 1586 (28 Eliz.), so also did Charles Howard of Effingham in 1597 and 1610. He had taken over Sir Thomas Carden's estate and castle, but his descendants had to transfer the estate to Sir Robert Clayton, who secured his return to one of the Bletchingley seats in 1689-90, and several times later . . .

And thus we reach the period which gave rise to Cobbett's description of the constituency as 'the vile rotten borough of Bletchingly.' It may be that Cobbett had formed his conclusion from the stories told by local gossips, or had read some of the reports of the Committee of the House upon the Petitions presented, in which corrupt practices of the most flagrant kind were found to be true, or he may have heard of the excessive zeal of the Rector, who lectured the parishioners upon the fearful consequences of voting contrary to his instructions. In any case Cobbett's denunciation, plain spoken as it was, was not too severe. The Rector's nominee succeeded at the poll, and was returned, but upon petition he was unseated for bribery, and the Rector had to kneel at the Bar of the House and sue for pardon. His prayer was granted on condition that he confessed his fault in church on the following Sunday. From the Committee's report

Cobbett might have learned much about the making of 'faggot votes' at the 1695 election.

. . . They told of the conveyance of burgage houses by word of mouth, without the payment of purchase money, and with the stipulation that the pretended vendor was to continue to receive the rents until that money was paid, and of other irregularities of the same kind. The Committee reported that the sitting Member had been duly elected, but their report was re-committed, further evidence was taken, the sitting Member was unseated, and the petitioner awarded the seat. Much more might be told of this and other attempts not merely to perpetrate jobs of the most flagrant character, but to mislead the different Committees of Investigation. It is stated that 'in the Clayton era the number of qualified voters were not many more than a dozen,' yet . . . forty-six burgesses, or pretended burgesses, recorded their votes. From 1783 down to disfranchisement of the Borough by the Reform Act of 1832 there were repeated instances of Members accepting the Stewardship either of the Chiltern Hundreds or of the Manor of East Hendred, County Berks, so that their nominees could secure the seat at bye-elections. There were no less than 15 of these occurrences within the period just named, some of them being caused by those who succeeded at the intermediate vacancies themselves vacating the seat in favour of those who participated in the 'borough-mongering' then prevalent. No wonder we are told that the inns set out their barrels of beer in the street free to all drinkers, and that the cobbled channels ran with beer. Yet, as a disfranchised Borough, Bletchingley ended with a flash of distinction; its last members were Thomas Hyde Villiers and Henry John, Viscount Palmerston, one of the Principal Secretaries of State, who succeeded to the seat vacated by Charles Tennyson who, having been doubly elected, decided to act as the representative of Stamford, in Lincolnshire.

J.E. Smith, The Parliamentary Representation of Surrey from 1290 to 1924 *(1927).*

11 · AT WORK

A variety of industrial and manufacturing processes were carried out in Surrey long before the Industrial Revolution took hold in the Midlands and northern England. Iron, glass, paper, cloth and gunpowder were amongst the county's products. Some of these activities took advantage of the copious supplies of water available from the county's rivers and streams, especially the Wey, Tillingbourne, Wandle and Hogsmill.

Making Paper at Byfleet

I went to see my Lord of St Alban's house at Byfleete, an old large building. Thence to the paper mills where I found them making a course white paper. They cull the rags which are linnen for white paper, woollen for brown; then they stamp them in troughs to a papp with pestles or hammers like the powder mills, then put it into a vessel of water, in which they dip a frame closely wyred with wyre as small as haire and as close as a weaver's reede; on this they take up the papp, the superfluous water draining through the wire; this they dextrously turning, shake out like a pancake on a smooth board between two pieces of flannel sucking out the moisture; then taking it out, they ply and dry it on strings, as they dry linen in the laundry; then dip it in alum water, lastly polish it and make it up in quires. They put some gum in the water in which they macerate the rags. The mark we find on the sheets is formed in the wyre.

John Evelyn, Diary, 1678. Paper was also made at Godalming, Chilworth, Ewell, Shottermill near Haslemere, and several other places in the county.

Chilworth Gunpowder

A gunpowder mill was established at Chilworth by the East India Company in 1626 and it continued to operate, with regular and sometimes fatally explosive interruptions, until 1920.

In this little pleasant Valley, the Springs serve not only to water the Grounds, but for the driving of 18 Powder Mills, 5 whereof were blown up in a little more than half a Years Time. 'Tis a little Commonwealth of Powder-makers, who are as black as Negroes.

Here is a Nursery of Earth for the making of Salt-Petre: There is also here a Boyling-House, where the Salt-Petre is made and shoots; a Corneing-House, all very well worth the seeing of the Ingenious. I had almost forgot the Brimstone Mill, and the Engine to search it. . .

The Powder-Mills of this Place were the first in England; and before they were erected, all our Gun-powder was imported at a great Expence from foreign Parts: Since which Time, the Place itself being so proper for such dangerous and useful Undertakings, the Mills have been farm'd out to several Hands, amongst the rest of the Gentlemen, Sir Polycarpus Wharton, Bart.

John Aubrey, The Natural History and Antiquities of Surrey *(begun c.1673).*

Here William Cobbett speaks his mind on gunpowder and that worst of all inventions, paper money! Paper was added to Chilworth's products in 1704.

Dorking, November 30 [1822]

I came over the high hill on the south of Guildford, and came down to Chilworth, and up the valley to Albury. I noticed, in my first Rural Ride, this beautiful valley, its hangers, its meadows, its hop-gardens, and its ponds. This valley of Chilworth has great variety, and is very pretty; but after seeing Hawkley, every other place loses in point of beauty and interest. This pretty valley of Chilworth has a run of water which comes out of the high hills, and which, occasionally, spreads into a pond; so that there is in fact a series of ponds connected by this run of water. This valley, which seems to have been created by a bountiful providence, as one of the choicest retreats of man; which seems formed for a scene of innocence and happiness, has been, by ungrateful man, so perverted as to make it instrumental in effecting two of the most damnable of purposes; in carrying into execution two of the most damnable inventions that ever sprang from the minds of man under the influence of the devil! Namely, the making of gunpowder and of banknotes! Here in this tranquil spot, where the nightingales are to be heard earlier and later in the year than in any other part of England; where the first bursting of the buds is seen in Spring, where no rigour of seasons can ever be felt; where everything seems formed for precluding the very thought of wickedness; here has the devil fixed on as one of the seats of his grand manufactory; and perverse and ungrateful man not only lends him his aid, but lends it cheerfully! As to the gunpowder, indeed, we might get over that. In some cases that may be innocently, and, when it sends the lead at the hordes that support a tyrant, meritoriously employed. The alders and the willows, therefore, one can see, without so much regret, turned into powder by the waters of this valley; but, the Bank-notes! To think that the springs which God has commanded to flow from the sides of these happy hills, for the comfort and delight of man; to think that these springs should be perverted into means of spreading misery over a whole nation; and that, too, under the base and hypocritical pretence of promoting its credit and maintaining its honour and its faith!

William Cobbett, Rural Rides *(1830)*.

Industrial Pollution – Surrey Style

In this extract the author bemoans the existence of the Chilworth Mills and the effects that the processes carried on there were having on the beautiful valley of the Tillingbourne River.

> Away: regard we yet again
> Nature's beauty,–and her bane:
> Alas! That man should e'er intrude
> Where all but he are glad and good,–
> Alas, for yonder fairy glen
> Nature's Eden, vext with men!
> Mammon, from those long white mills

With fogey steam the prospect fills;
Chimneys red with sulph'rous smoke
Blight those hanging groves of oak;
And sylvan Quiet's gentle scenes,
List – to the clatter of machines.
Yet more, in yonder rural dell
Where sylphs and fauns might love to dwell,
Among those alders, by the stream
Stealing on with silver gleam,
Blackened huts, set wide apart,
Grind their dark grain for murder's mart,
Or bursting with explosive might
Rage, and roar, and blast, and blight.

Martin Tupper, 'St. Martha's' (1849). Tupper lived at nearby Albury.

Explosion at Molesey

Saturday, 19 [July] About two this afternoon, a place called the Dust-house, belonging to Mr. Norman's gunpowder mill, at Moulsey, in Surrey, blew up, and killed one man, who was barrelling up the gunpowder. It is reckoned there were about 30 barrels of powder containing about 100lb. weight. The building was blown into thousands of pieces, and carried a great way; the poor man's body was torn into so many pieces, there was no finding them, or half his bones. Seven or eight great elms, that stood near this room, were tore up by the roots, and many others shattered, and several adjacent buildings terribly tore; a building about 30 yards from it, which contained about the same quantity of gunpowder, had its roof beat in, and a man at work received a slight blow on the back of his neck, by a piece of timber, but the powder remained safe. The windows of several neighbouring houses were broke, and some of the tiles blown off houses at some distance, by the force of the shock. The houses for many miles about were shaken by the explosion.

Annual Register, 1754.

Cloths of Guildford

Woollen cloth was produced in a number places in the county during the Middle Ages and, although the industry declined rapidly in the seventeenth century, it did not finally cease until the Victorian period.

By Henry III's reign Guildford had become a wealthy town and its prosperity derived largely from the wool trade. The Cistercians, who founded Waverley Abbey in 1128, introduced commercial wool production into west Surrey. The downs and commons provided rough grazing; and the sheep were shorn, the fleeces spun into yarn and the yarn woven into cloth in the villages and farms around. The new cloth would then go to Guildford or one of the other nearby towns to be finished.

The first finishing process was 'fulling' – pummelling the cloth in a vat of water to produce a nap and also to clean it; fuller's earth was used to remove the natural grease so that the wool would take the dye. At first fulling was done by trampling the cloth in wooden tubs, but was then mechanised with the introduction of fulling mills, where large wooden mallets, powered by water-wheels, hammered the wool. One of the earliest fulling mills in England was built by Henry III at Guildford in 1251 and by the end of the Middle Ages at least four were operating in the Millmead area.

The next process was dyeing, frequently with woad to produce 'Guildford blue' cloth. (There are records of dyehouses near the Town Bridge in Elizabethan times.) The piece of cloth, hot and wet from the dye-vat, would be hooked to racks or tenter-frames to dry evenly: there were racks at Millmead by 1394 and others gave their name to Racks Close. The nap would then be brushed up with teazels and sheared off to a smooth surface. The finished cloth, known technically as a kersey, was then ready for sale and much of it went for export to the Continent.

All stages of the manufacture would be superintended by the 'clothier', the entrepreneur who would handle the sale of the finished product and reap a considerable profit. Nevertheless, this profit seems to have been thought insufficient by some.

As early as 1391 an Act of Parliament complained that unscrupulous clothiers were ruining the reputation of 'cloths of

Guildford' by stretching the cloth before drying. This artificially lengthened the piece, but the cloth would shrink back again if ever the customer got it wet. Dishonest stretching continued to be a problem for the next three hundred years and many blamed it for the final decline of the west Surrey wool trade.

Matthew Alexander, Guildford: A Short History, *revised edition (1992).*

The Croydon Colliers

If the descriptions of old writers are to be depended upon, Croydon, in the days of Elizabeth and even later, was not a very desirable place for a residence. Its principal industry was charcoal burning. Names still left, such as Woodside, Croham Hurst, Selhurst, etc., show that it was surrounded by woods, the trees being of the most desirable kind for producing charcoal, which, in the absence of coal, was the fuel principally used. The streets of Croydon at that period are described as 'dark hollow ways and very dirty, the houses with wooden steps and chiefly inhabited by colliers,' as the charcoal burners were termed. A poem, written in 1622 by Patrick Hanney, says:

> In midst of these stands Croydon clothed in black,
> In a low bottom smoke of all these hills,
> Which from their tops still in abundance trills,
> The unpaved lanes with muddy mire them fills.
>
> And those who there inhabit, sorting well,
> With such a place, do negroes seem;
> Besmeared with soot and breathing pitchy smoke,
> Which (save themselves) a living wight would choke.

Many of these charcoal burners, however, were men in affluent circumstances, and the charities of Croydon bear testimony to their liberality; they were also men possessing influence which often stood them in good stead. At the old farm of Colliers' Water, in the days of Archbishop Grindall, lived a collier whose trade brought down upon him the wrath of the great prelate. The collier was sighted at Westminster to answer for the annoyance caused to residents of the palace by the foulness of the smoke. The old collier supplied the various City Guilds, and made his case known to the Aldermen, who, perceiving that if his trade was interfered with, their cooks would not be able to get the dinners for the city feasts, resolved to help him. When the trial came on, it was pleaded that charcoal was indispensable to the comfort of the inhabitants, that it could not be produced without smoke, and that the collier had only carried on his business fairly as all colliers must do, and the result was he came off triumphant. One outcome of the trial was a play, said to have been written by Shakespeare in his younger days, and entitled, 'The Saucy Collier of Croydon and the Devil,' the latter representing the primate who put his own personal comfort before the general interests of the citizens. An old song called 'The Collier of Croydon,' was very popular, and ran as follows:

> It is said that in Croydon there did sometyme dwell
> A Colyer that did all other Colyers excel;
> For his riches thys Colyer might have been a knight,
> But in the order of Knighthood he had no delight.
> Would God all our knights did mind coling no more
> Than thys Collyer did Knighting, as is sayd before;
> For when none but pore Collyers did with coles mell,
> At a reasonable price did their Coles sell;
> But synce our Knight Collyers have had the first sale,
> We have pay'd much money, and had few sacks to tale.
> A lode, that late years for a royal was sold,
> Wyl cost now sixteen shillings of sylver or gold.
> God grant these men grace their polling to repayne,
> Or else bring them back to theyr old state agayne;
> And especially the Collyer that at Collyer's Water doth dwell,
> For we think he is kin to the Collyer of Hell.

The Surrey Magazine, May, 1903. Charcoal also fuelled the Wealden iron furnaces and was used in the manufacture of glass, particularly in the Chiddingfold, Hambledon and Alfold areas. Here was the centre of English glass-making until the late sixteenth century. At one time so many oak trees were being felled for charcoal that steps were taken to restrict its production, amidst fears that there would be a shortage of good oak for shipbuilding.

Gatton

Because of the hugely varied geology of Surrey, the minerals dug, quarried or mined in the county have been equally diverse. Chalk, sandstone, flint, sand, clay, gravel, iron ore and hearthstone or firestone have all been extracted at various times over the centuries.

It is famous for a white Free-stone Quarry, wherein are under Ground several Meanders; it is soft, and endures the Fire admirably well in Winter, but neither Sun nor Air: The Stone lies about fourteen Foot deep, and from the Mouth of the Quarry proceeds a thick Mist in hot Weather. This Stone is much used by Chymists, Bakers, Glass-Houses, &c.

John Aubrey The Natural History and Antiquities of Surrey *(started c.1673). The miles of caverns and underground passages found in many parts of East Surrey are the legacy of this now defunct industry.*

Broom-squires

I have given examples of some of the county's substantial manufactures, but there were also many small-scale 'cottage industries', including the activities of the 'broom-squires', which I find particularly interesting.

A cottage industry that still survives in this neighbourhood is the making of birch and heath brooms. As no cast-iron or machine-made substitute for these useful things has yet appeared, let us hope that they may still remain. Their safety is probably in their cheapness, for the price in the country, buying direct from the maker, is three and sixpence a dozen for birch and half-a-crown a dozen for heath. The materials cost the makers very little; often much less than the rightful owner of the birches and handle stuff intends or is aware of, and they are quickly and easily made.

Among the broom-squarers or broom-squires there have always been some very rough characters. Two generations ago they were rougher still, for then their haunts among the heathy wastes had not been invaded by the builder, or by civilising influences. But there are many good, honest, hard-working men among them. One, who for many years has supplied me with a regular yearly 'four dozen birch and two dozen heath,' I am sorry to know is now past work.

The birch spray is not used fresh. It is put aside to dry and toughen for some months. Then they 'break birch for brooms.' A faggot is opened, and the spray is broken by hand to the right size and laid in bundles. Breaking birch is often women's work. The 'bonds' that fasten the spray on to the handle are of hazel or withy, split and shaved with the knife into thick ribbons. They are soaked in water to make them lissom. There is usually a little pool of water near the broom-maker's shed, where the bonds are soaked.

The broom-squarer gathers up the spray round the end of the stick, sitting in front of a heavy fixed block to which the further end of a bond is made fast. He pushes the near end of the bond into the butts of the spray, nearly at a right angle from him, pulling it tight as it goes. When he has wound up to the length of the bond, the end is released and pushed into the work. Heath brooms have two bonds; birch, which are much longer, have three. A hole is bored between the strands of spray and through the stick, and a peg is driven tightly through, so that the spray cannot slip off the stick. The rough butts are then trimmed off, and the broom is complete.

They generally work in thatched sheds, the thatch commonly of heather. In old days it was usual to keep their money in some hole in the thatch inside; they considered it safer than keeping it in the cottages. The man would put up his hand into a place something like a bird's nest, and there was the money. An old friend, who knew their ways well, told me he had known of a sum of between three and four hundred pounds being kept in this way.

Gertrude Jekyll, Old West Surrey (1904).

Sabine Baring-Gould based his novel The Broom-Squire *on the unusual way of life of these people, many of whom lived as squatters in the Devil's Punch Bowl at Hindhead. For the framework of the book, he used the tale of the infamous murder of the 'unknown sailor', which took place at Hindhead in 1786. In the factual version the victim was alone when he was robbed and murdered by three footpads, who were latter hanged for the crime. However, in Baring-Gould's version the murder victim was accompanied by a baby, who survived the ordeal.*

The Broom-Squire and the boy were on their way up the hill that led towards the habitation of the former. The evening had closed in. But that mattered not to them, for they knew their way and had not far to go.

The road mounted continuously, first a slight incline over sand sprinkled with Scotch pine, and then more rapidly to the range of hills that culminates in Leith Hill and Hind Head, and breaks into the singular cones entitled The Devil's Jumps.

After the road had ascended some way, all trees disappeared. The scenery was as wild and desolate as any in Scotland. On all sides heathery slopes, in the evening light a broken patch of sand showed white, almost phosphorescent, through contrast with the black ling. A melancholy bird piped. Otherwise all was still. The richly wooded weald, with here and there a light twinkling on it, lay far below, stretching to Lewes. When the high road nearly reached the summit it was carried in a curve along the edge of a strange depression, a vast basin in the sand-hills, sinking three hundred feet to a marshy bottom full of oozing springs. This is termed the Devil's Punch Bowl. The modern road is carried at a lower level, and is banked up against the steep incline. The old road was not thus protected and ran considerably higher . . .

'Here's the spot where the turn comes that leads off the road to my house. Mind where you walk, and don't roll over down the Punch Bowl; it's all bog at the bottom.'

'There's no light anywhere,' observed the boy.

'No – no windows look this way. You can't say if a house is alive or dead from here.'

'How long have you had your place in the Punch Bowl, Bideabout?'

'I've heard say my grandfather was the first squatter. But the Rocliffes, Boxalls, Snellings, and Nashes, will have it they're older. What do I care so long as I have the best squat of the lot.'

That the reader may understand the allusions, a word or two must be allowed in explanation of the settlements in the Punch Bowl.

At some unknown date squatters settled in the Punch Bowl, at a period when it was as wild and solitary a region as any in England. They enclosed portions of the slope. They built themselves hovels; they pastured their sheep, goats, cattle, on the side of the Punch Bowl, and they added to their earnings the profits of a trade they monopolised – that of making and selling brooms.

On the lower slopes of the range grew coppices of Spanish chestnut, and rods of this wood served admirably for broom handles. The heather, when long and wiry and strong, covered with its harsh leafage and myriad hard knobs that were to burst into flower, answered for the brush.

On account of this manufacture, the squatters in the Punch Bowl went by the designation of Broom-Squires. They provided with brooms every farm and gentleman's house, nay, every cottage for many miles round. A waggon-load of these besoms was often purchased, and the supply lasted some years.

The Broom-Squires were an independent people. They used the cut turf from the common for fuel and the farmers were glad to carry away the potash as manure for their fields.

Another business supplemented farming and broom-making. That was holly-cutting and selling. The Broom-Squires on the approach of Christmas scattered over the country, and wherever they found holly trees and bushes laden with berries, without asking permission, regardless of prohibition, cut, and then when they had gathered a cartload, would travel with it to London or Guildford, to attend the Christmas market.

At the present date there are eight squatter families in the Punch Bowl, three belong to the clan of Boxall, three to that of Snelling, and two to the less mighty clan of Nash. At the time of which I write one of the best built houses and the most fertile patches of land was in the possession of the young man Jonas Kink, commonly known as Bideabout.

Jonas was a bachelor. His father was dead and his sister had married one of the Rocliffes. She was his senior by many years. He lived alone in his fairly substantial house, and his sister came in when she was able to put it tidy for him and to do some necessary cooking. He was regarded as close-fisted though young, about twenty-three years. Hitherto no girl had caught his fancy, or had caught it sufficiently to induce him to take one to wife.

'Tell'y what,' said his sister, 'you'll be nothing else but an old hudger (bachelor).'

This was coming to be a general opinion. Jonas Kink has a heart for money, and for that only. He sneered at girls and flouted them. It was said that Jonas would marry no girl save for her money, and that a moneyed girl might pick and choose herself, and such as she would most assuredly not make selection of Bideabout. Consequently he was fore-doomed to be a 'hudger.'

'What's that?' suddenly exclaimed the Broom-Squire, who led the way along a footpath on the side of the steep slope.

'It's a dead sheep, I fancy, Bideabout.'

'A dead sheep–I wonder if it be mine. Hold hard, what's that noise?'

'It's like a babe's cry,' said the boy. 'Oh, lawk, if it be dead and ha' become a wanderer! I shu'd never have the pluck to go home alone.'

'Get along with your wanderers. It's arrant nonsense. I don't believe a word of it.'

'But there is the crying again. It is near at hand. Oh, Bideabout! I be terrified!'

'I'll strike a light. I'm not sure about this being a dead sheep.'
Something lay on the path, catching what little light came from the sky.

Jonas stooped and plucked some dry grass. Then he got out his tinderbox and struck, struck, struck.

The boy's eyes were on the flashing sparks. He feared to look elsewhere. Presently the tinder was ignited, and the Broom-Squire blew it and held dry grass haulms to the glowing embers till a blue flame danced up, becoming yellow, and burst into a flare.

Cautiously Jonas approached the prostrate figure and waved the flaming grass above it, while sparks flew about and fell over it.

The boy, shrinking behind the man, looked timidly before him, and uttered a cry as the yellow flare fell over the object and illuminated a face.

'I thought as much,' said the Broom-Squire. 'What else could he expect? Them there chaps ha' murdered him . . .'

S. Baring-Gould, The Broom-Squire (1896).

13 · AT PLAY

Surrey has always had much to offer in terms of sport and entertainment, attracting thousands of Londoners each weekend. The county became the playground of the metropolis once the railways had brought its towns, villages and countryside within easy reach.

A Rambler's Paradise

Surrey is second to no county in England for a combination of allurements which make it a delightful holiday ground. There is no part of it which is not within easy reach of London, and yet it is rich in wild heaths and lonely byways as in picturesque hamlets that still sleep in the peace of security among their unchanged environments of centuries ago. Nature seems so to have arranged its physical charms as to give variety in perfection, so rapidly can its delightful scenes be made to pass before the eye. In a short day's ramble one may walk by plashy water-meadows and sandy heights, over wind-swept moorland and in drowsy lanes, on airy uplands and in fern-clothed valleys, through dense forest and busy hop-gardens. Hardly a village is there that has not its ancient church, a mine of interest to the antiquary; its old-world inn by the village green, fit subject for a Morland; some visible relic of its ancient civilisation, or quaint piece of folk-lore recalled by gaffer gossip or lingering custom.

Duncan Moul & Gibson Thompson, Picturesque Surrey *(1902).*

Early Cricket

This is claimed to be the earliest documentary reference to the game and dates to 1598.

John Derrick, gent. one of the queene's majestie's coroners of the county of Surrey aged 59 saith this land beforemention'd lett to John Parvish, Innholder, deceased, that he knew it for fifty yeares or more. It lay waste and was used and occupied by the inhabitants of Guldeford to saw timber in and for sawpits and for makinge of frames of timber for the said inhabitantes. When he was a scholler in the free school of Guldeford, he and several of his fellowes did runne and play there at crickett and other plaies. And also that the same was used for the baytinge of beares in the said towne, until the said John Parvish did inclose the said parcell of land. It lay between the garden sometymes Thomas Northall on the north part, and the highway leadinge through the north town ditch on the south.

Russell's History of Guildford *(1801).*

Cricket at Molesey

On Wednesday last a Cricket Match was play'd on Molesey Hurst in Surrey, between Eleven Surrey Men and Eleven of Middlesex, at which the Prince of Wales was present. It was a very hard Match, but at last the Surrey Men got it by three Notches; and his Royal Highness order'd a Guinea to each Man for their great Dexterity, &c.

Just as his Royal Highness was returning from that Match to Hampton Court, a Hare was put up among the Tents in the Camp, which being pursued by several Soldiers, &c. she took the Water, and several Horse Grenadiers being also in Pursuit in their Jack-Boots, jumped in after her and catched her before she had swam quite into the middle of the Thames; who all laying claim to the Prize, a Water Battle ensued, before they could bring their Booty on Shoar, which afforded his Royal Highness and the Nobility much Diversion.

Cutting from an unidentified newspaper dated 1733.

A Dangerous Game

On Monday last the great Match at Cricket, so long depending between the Gentlemen of Hambledon, in Hants, called 'Squire Lamb's Club, and the Gentlemen of Chertsey, was played on Laleham Borough. Chertsey went in first, and got 48 Notches, Hambledon got 76. Second Innings, Chertsey headed 87, John Edmonds and Thomas Baldwin turned the Game, by getting upwards of 40 Notches: Time expired, and they postponed it till the next Morning, when Chertsey went in and got 12 Notches; Hambledon went in, three out for four Notches, the next five got, won the Game. Chertsey had three men much hurt, and Hambledon had two, Mr Steward having his finger broke, and his knee sprained. On this Match great Sums of Money were depending. During the Cricket Match a Gentleman of Fortune at Weybridge was taken up by a Warrant for a Bastard Child, which caused a great deal of Diversion; the Gentleman drew his Sword on the Officer, and afterwards presented a Pistol, and went off in Triumph.

Unidentified newspaper cutting dated 1764.

Lumpy Stevens

Having now described the best of my native players, I proceed to their opponents; and the foremost man of all must stand the well-known bowler Lumpy, whose real name was Stevens. He was a Surrey man, and lived with Lord Tankerville. Beyond all the men within my recollection, Lumpy would bowl the greatest number of length balls in succession. His pace was much faster than Lord Beauclerc's, but he wanted his Lordship's general knowledge of the game. In those days it was the custom for the party going from home to pitch their own wickets; and here it was that Lumpy, whose duty it was to attend to this, always committed an error. He would invariably choose the ground where his balls would shoot, instead of selecting a spot to bowl against; which would have materially increased the difficulty to the hitter, seeing that so many more would be caught out by the mounting of the ball. As nothing, however, delighted the old man like bowling a wicket down with a shooting ball, so he would sacrifice the other chances to the glory of that achievement. Many a time have I seen our general twig this prejudice in the old man when matched against us, and chuckle at it. But I believe it was almost the only mistake he ever made professional, or even moral, for he was a most simple and amiable creature. Yes – one other he committed, and many the day after was the joke remembered against him. One of our matches having been concluded early in the day, a long, raw-boned devil of a countryman came up and offered to play any one of the 22 at single wicket for five pounds. Old Nyren told Lumpy it would be five pounds easily earned, and persuaded him to accept the challenge. Lumpy, however, would not stake the whole sum himself, but offered a pound of the money, and the rest was subscribed. The confident old bowler made the countryman go in first, for he thought to settle his business in a twink: but the fellow having an arm as long as a hop-pole reached out at Lumpy's balls, bowl what length he might; so he slashed and thrashed away in the most ludicrous style, hitting his balls all over the field, and always up in the air, and he made an uncommon number of runs from this prince of bowlers before he could get him out; – and, egad! He beat him! – for when Lumpy went in, not being a good batter, while the other was a very fast bowler, all along the ground, and strait to the wicket, he knocked him out presently; the whole ring roaring with laughter, and the astounded old bowler swearing he would never play another single match as long as he lived – an oath, I am sure, he religiously observed, for he was confounded crest-fallen. Lumpy was a short man, round shouldered and stout. He had no trick about him, but was as plain as a pike-staff in all his dealings.

John Nyren, The Cricketers of My Time *(1832), new edition edited by Ashley* Mote *(1998).*

County Cricket

Godalming is a decent sort of town, with a rather fine church, pleasantly situated, and in the God's acre thereof lies the body of Manning, the historian of the county, above which, says my old Guide, is a 'headstone with an epitaph upon it, though he expressly forbade his family and friends to erect any monument to him.' I presently discovered a newsroom, with that day's papers, wherein I quietly ensconced myself, while Ned made a pilgrimage to the tomb of Manning, and 'My Uncle' went to call on a friend in the town, respecting whom the only certain intelligence I can give is, that he didn't ask him to lunch.

The cricket match, which was played on the Broadwater Ground, was very good, said to have been one of the best of the season, and was very numerously attended, several carriages full of youth and beauty, and one handsome, tall, and pensive young man, in a complete suit of black velvet (and who struck me as being possibly the ghost of Hamlet, though why he should select a cricket-field for his walk I couldn't imagine, and didn't like to ask), adorning the ground.

It was the second day's game, and would, weather permitting, be concluded on the morrow: we afterwards heard, with pride in our county's skill, that Surrey was the victor. On the ground we learnt the death of Lillywhite, the well known Sussex player, and introducer of 'round' bowling: he fell a victim to the prevailing epidemic, at his house at Islington, and was in his sixty-fourth year.

M.C. Turner, A Saunter Through Surrey *(1857)*.

Shovell Groate

Thomas Bennett late of Catterham, 1 Dec. 1661 and often times before and since, illegally allowed . . . in his house there various unlawful games, ' . . . Cardes Dice Tables and Shovell groate' for his monetary advantage and profit, to the great disturbance . . . of the neighbours, in evil example . . . against the statute . . . and against the peace . . .

Surrey Quarter Sessions, January 1662. As a 'groate' was worth fourpence (a little less than 2p), 'Shovell groate' must have been a rather expensive early version of 'shove-ha'penny', the old halfpenny being worth not quite a quarter of 1p!

Pot Pourri from a Surrey Garden

Miles of pram in the wind and Pam in the gorse track,
   Coco-nut smell of the broom, and a packet of Weights
Press'd in the sand. The thud of a hoof on a horse-track—
     A horse-riding horse for a horse-track—
     Conifer county of Surrey approached
   Through remarkable wrought-iron gates.

Over your boundary now, I wash my face in a bird-bath,
   Then which path shall I take? that over there by the pram?
Down by the pond! or — yes, I will take the slippery third path,
     Trodden away with gym shoes,
     Beautiful fir-dry alley that leads
   To the bountiful body of Pam.

Pam, I adore you, Pam, you great big moutainous sports girl,
   Whizzing them over the net, full of the strength of five:
That old Malverian brother, you zephyr and khaki shorts girl,
     Although he's playing for Woking,
     Can't stand up
   To your wonderful backhand drive.

See the strength of her arm, as firm and hairy as Hendren's;
   See the size of her thighs, the pout of her lips as, cross,
And full of a pent-up strength, she swipes at the rhododendrons,
     Lucky the rhododendrons,
     And flings her arrogant love-lock
   Back with a petulant toss.

Over the redolent pinewoods, in at the bathroom casement,
   One fine Saturday, Windlesham bells shall call:
Up the Butterfield aisle rich with Gothic enlacement,
     Licensed now for embracement,
     Pam and I, as the organ
   Thunders over you all.

John Betjeman, Collected Poems *(1966)*.

Race Days

In the eighteenth and early nineteenth century there were racecourses at Reigate, Croydon, Guildford and Egham, all of which became notorious for thieves, frauds and unruly characters. In 1875 the first enclosed 'park' course in Britain was opened at Sandown Park, Esher. Now the calibre of the racegoers could be controlled.

Aug 25th 1813 – EGHAM RACES – Smolensko, the famous racer, drew a company unprecedented in the course. The visitors were so eager to get a sight of him, that crowds waited at the stable door; and after the race, Sir C. Bunbury desired that the company might be gratified with a full view of him. He was placed in a circle opposite the royal stand for the Queen and Princesses to view, and afterwards in other parts of the course.

The first was the Magna Charta stakes of 50 guineas each, for three years old colts, to carry 8st. 5lb. The winner of the Derby or Oaks to carry 5lb extra.

Sir C. Bunbury's bl. C. Smolensko, 1

Duke of York's c. by Giles, out of Venture's dam, 2

Smolensko was said to have been short of work, and he was the favourite at seven to four only. Goodison, who rode him, kept up the appearance of a race with Chiffney, who rode the Duke's colt, till opposite the royal stand, within 20 yards of the winning-post, when he slacked the reins, and Smolensko got a length in a moment, and won in a canter.

Edinburgh Annual Register, *1813*.

Epsom Races

In Surrey today only Epsom remains of the once famous (and infamous) 'open' racecourses.

Towards the evening we bade them Adieu! And took horse; being resolved that, instead of the race which fails us, we would go to Epsom. When we came there we could hear of no lodging the town so full; but which was better, I went towards Ashted and there we got a lodging in a little hole we could not stand upright in.

Samuel Pepys, Diary, 25 July, 1663.

Derby Day

THE DERBY – On Thursday, the day 'big with the fate' of the Derby, the road resounded with the dashing of carriages, and the rush of horsemen; barouches, chaises, gigs, and carts, contended with each other, and became all but lost in inextricable confusion. It was amusing (as far dust would permit) to watch the crash of carriages, the upsetting of gigs, the disasters of amibitious carts, with kitchen-chairs in them in lieu of seats – to see the puffing, the blowing, the whipping, the spurring, the brilliant costume of the fashionable crowd, and the great gaudy trimmings of the more humble votaries of pleasure. To avert the rays of the sun, that rendered the road like the Egyptian Desert, the ladies resorted to all those means which they are accustomed to command; and many of the gentlemen called forth the derision of the crowd by appearing in green veils. The course itself, contrasted with what it was on the first two days, exhibited a brilliant and crowded appearance. It was lined by carriages from Tattenham-corner to the winning post, but the greater number were equipages of an equivocal rank, and stage-coaches and carts had possession of some of the principal points of view. Next to the grand stand and the Course, the great attraction was the betting-ring on the hill, where all the principal sportsmen, on horseback, were collected in a dense mass, laying wagers of enormous amount, in order to make small profits to a certainty, and giving or taking the odds in every variety of combination, in order to secure an advantageous book.

The Derby this year had, after a variety of fluctuations, been assigned, as a certainty, to a horse of the Earl of Jersey – Riddlesworth – which had won all its previous races in a style deemed equal, if not superior, to any that was ever in the field. The odds against him daily grew less; and on Wednesday went as high as six to four against a field of 20 horses.

Annual Register, *1831. As proof, if it were needed, that there is no such thing as a certainty, Riddlesworth was beaten into second place by an outsider!*

*Here an American experiences the delights of Epsom Downs on
Derby Day in the 1930s.*

As our taxi reached the station, I saw signs calling attention to 'Special
trains to Epsom and return, first class five shillings, third class three,
class not guaranteed'. This meant that, having bought a first-class
ticket, I might have to be content with third-class accommodation; so,
as I usually travel third anyway, I took third-class tickets, got excellent
seats in a train that was just pulling out, and in little over half an hour
reached the Downs. It was not yet eleven o'clock, but already there
was an immense crowd, people coming from all points of the compass
and by thousands – quiet, orderly, well-behaved, plain people, intent,
like myself, on having a good time. Some had been on the Downs for
several days, living in motors, tents, in and under wagons, in the
neighborhood – living any old way; for be it understood that,
although there is but one Derby Day and the 'Derby' is only one of
several races run on that day, the Derby races are run for the best part
of a week, and are followed by the 'Oaks' and other races. Englishmen
live for sport, for life in the open, to a degree quite unknown to us;
therein, as in most things, they are wiser than we.

The Downs Station is about a mile from the grandstand, which is,
more or less, the objective of everyone who goes to the Derby. Five
minutes after leaving the station we came upon a group of Welsh
singers – singing very well too. On a sheet on the ground in front of
them were a number of small coins, for the most part copper, but with
a few sixpences and shillings, the latter doubtless intended to suggest
the singers' own appraisement of the value of their concert. We had
only listened for a moment when an old hag, a gypsy, came up and
wanted to tell my fortune. She told me I should come into money, and
for half a crown would tell me when and how. Meantime a man
offered to guess my wife's age and weight. These matters being a
profound secret, he was received with withering scorn; I really pitied
him. Sellers of tips on the races were on every hand. Old 'Arry has
been backing the winners for years, had taken his own advice
yesterday, and made a pot of money, offered much better advice to-
day, and, to show how little he cared for money, lit a cigar with a ten
shilling note (stage money). Another man, an accomplice, rushing up,
seemingly paid him a pound for some secret information contained in

a sealed envelope, and disappeared. 'Arry had only one more left; this he would dispose of for ten shillings to effect a quick sale; he had important business elsewhere and was in an 'urry. A man with a small collapsible table before him was doing card tricks; the time-honoured shell game was going on under one's very eyes, and a very primitive sort of roulette everywhere. 'Violets, lovely violets, sixpence; well, then, tuppence; take 'em and God bless you.' The crowd increases. Hawkers abound, seeking to sell toys, souvenirs, trash of all kinds; one wonders who would buy the stuff and burden themselves all day with it. Multiply the side shows of a country circus by a thousand, and you will have some idea of the Downs on Derby Day.

A. Edward Newton, Derby Day and Other Adventures (c.1935).

More Horsy Business - The Leaping Butcher

The metropolis and its surrounding district produces some of the best and hardiest riders in England; and I have seen and heard of one or two instances which would bear comparison with many of the break-neck feats of the sister kingdom. There is a butcher named Selmes, of Godstone, who is noted for his nerve, and the extraordinary knack he has of making any horse jump: cart-horse or race-horse is all the same to him when once on their back; go they must at what ever he puts them at, and no horse is ever in his hands a month without becoming a jumper. With a snaffle bridle and the buckle of the rein in one hand, the head quite loose, a good ash stick in the right hand, and one spur on the left heel, he charges gates, stiles, hedges, or brooks; and refuse they dare not, for the ash plant is sure to catch them on the side of the head if they offer to turn to the right or to the left. They may fall if they please, and they very often do at first; but they soon become quite as much afraid of doing that as refusing. The man himself is as active as a cat, and seldom gets hurt. There is a very high and pointed barred gate, leading off the common into the paddock belonging to the kennel; I should think it could not be less than four feet nine inches; and one day in the summer, while up at the kennel, chatting to some of the people, he began to show off his horse, by jumping over some hurdles, and a rail round a stack. He then, without much of a run, rode at this gate, and over he went; but the horse struck the top of the spikes with his hind feet, and broke two of them; and at the same time, one of his stirrup leathers gave way. This not pleasing him, he turned the animal short round, and brought him back over it again, and then a third time out of the field over it again, both the last times with only one stirrup, and going at least a foot higher than the gate. The horse was afterwards bought for £100 by Sir E. Antrobus.

Sporting Magazine, *1839*.

The Great Steeple Chase

The sporting match between Captain Manton and Mr. Malpas, for 200 guineas, took place this morning, from Mount Sorrel House, Surrey, to Frimley Covers, a distance of eleven milles of difficult country. To make the nearest way there were many perilous leaps, which the horses cleared, with their riders, in fine style, and left the greater part of a field of sportsmen who accompanied them. The competitors kept together to the Bottle Cover, when they separated, and skirted it at opposite angles, and at the ridge of the hills, three miles from Frimley, the race became very interesting. It was neck or nothing down the hills, with leaps nearly six feet. But the most interesting part was the leap at a rivulet of fourteen feet, which might have been avoided by taking a route of a quarter of a mile. Both horses cleared it in gallant style, and the race came to the speed of the horses up the hill to the Cover, and Captain Manton won it by two hundred yards, in thirty-four minutes.

Annual Register, *1821*.

Pugilism

Boxing matches before the introduction of the Marquis of Queensberry's rules were usually long and bloody affairs, fought in the open in front of vast crowds. Molesey Hurst, where Hurst Park Racecourse was later built, was a popular location for these fights. The area is now occupied by a housing estate.

A boxing match took place on Tuesday at Moulsey Hurst, between two men named Turner and Curtis, the former of whom had not before contested a prize battle. The contest extended to 68 rounds and lasted an hour and 28 minutes, during which Turner received two or three severe blows only, while his antagonist was dreadfully beaten, and at the close completely exhausted. He was put to bed in a most deplorable state, at an inn, in Hampton, and there died of the injuries he had received.

Newspaper cutting dated 1816.

> To see the Hurst with tents encamped on
> Look around the scene at Hampton.
> 'Tis life to cross the laden ferry
> with boon companions, wild and merry,
> And see the ring upon the Hurst
> With carts encircled – hear the burst
> At distance, of the eager crowd.

Peter Corocan, 'The Fancy' (1820).

BOXING – A battle took place at Moulsey Hurst on Tuesday between Cabbage and Parish. The battle commenced before one o'clock, and was soon decided by a stunning blow at the start. Belcher and Harmer seconded Cabbage, and Tom Owen and Josh Hudson picked Parish up. Betting was 6 to 4 on Parish, the heaviest man – Round 1. Cabbage hit short, and was well parried; but he made another rush, and place a right-handed blow upon his adversary's eye, rather out of distance, and which flushed it. Parish retreated. But his man would not leave him, and he floored him by a heavy left-handed blow upon the throat. 3 to 1 on Cabbage. Round 2. Parish made play by bolting in, when he hit away at random, and was hit again and thrown. Round 3. A good fighting round, and Parish made some fine parries, and seemed to be recovering. He made a good stand in a rally and was then thrown. Round 4. Parish was again thrown. Round 5. In this round Parish was hit to sleep with the right hand, and then thrown with great dexterity. In the 6th and 7th he only stood up to be slaughtered, and a very proper interference took place to avoid any chance of slaughter. It lasted six minutes only.

From a newspaper cutting dated 1822.

Freedom of the Open Road

The 'safety' bicycle was invented in the 1880s and soon Surrey became a weekend mecca for thousands of cycling enthusiasts intent on escaping the smog of London.

The Portsmouth Road, from London to Ripley, has, any time these last twenty years, been the most frequented by cyclists of any road in England. The 'Ripley Road,' as it is generally known among wheel-men, is throughout the year, but more especially in the spring and summer months, alive with cycles and noisy with ringing of cycle-bells. On Saturday afternoons, and on fine Sundays, an almost inconceivable number take a journey down these twenty-three miles from London, and back again in the evening; calling at the 'Angel,' at Ditton, on the way, and taking tea at their Mecca the 'Anchor,' at Ripley. The road is excellent for cycling, but so also are a number of others, equally accessible, around London, and it must be acknowledged that the 'Ripley Road' is as much favoured by a single freak of fashion in cycling, and as illogically, as a particular walk in Hyde Park is affected by Society on Sundays. But in cycling circles (apt phrase!) it is quite the correct thing to be seen at Ditton or at Ripley on a Sunday, and every one who is any one in that sport and pastime, be-devilled as it is now-a-days with shady professionalism and the transparently subsidized performances of the makers' amateurs, must be there. The 'Ripley Road,' now-a-days, is, in fact, the stalking-ground of self-advertising long-distance riders, of cliquey and boisterous club-men, and of the immodest women who wear breeches awheel. The tourist, and the man who only has a fancy for the cycle as a means of healthful exercise, and does not join the membership of a club, give the 'Ripley Road' a wide berth.

The frequenters of this road became in 1894 such an unmitigated nuisance and source of danger to the public in passing through Kingston-upon-Thames, that the local bench of magistrates were obliged to institute proceedings against a number of cyclists for furious driving, and riding machines without lights or bells. According to the evidence given by an inspector of police, no fewer than twenty thousand cyclists passed through Kingston on Whit Sunday, 1894.

Charles G. Harper, The Portsmouth Road *(1895).*

The World's First Motor Racing Circuit

Among these early devotees of motoring, with both the money and the courage necessary to indulge it, was Mr. H.F. Locke King, builder of the famous Mena House Hotel near Cairo, and owner of an estate near Weybridge, who actually in September, 1905, took his 70 h.p. Itala across Italy to attend the road-racing at Brescia. It had been an exciting journey. The car was driven first into a mountain on one side of the road so severely damaging its steering that it could with difficulty be kept off the precipice on the other side, and would only consent to take its occupants as far as Turin, sounding its horn triumphantly the while peasants sought refuge in adjacent ditches. To Brescia at last they came, to find the race over, but in their inn that evening the Italians who had competed recounted them the story, dwelling with especial exultation on their own victories and with derision on the failures of the English, the unsportsmanlike English who had neither the practice nor machines to bring them home a prize. Mr Locke King said nothing, possibly because there was nothing to be said to a sad truth, and went back to his house at Weybridge; a little later Mr Julian Orde, secretary of the R.A.C., suggested that a circular English track be built where cars might be watched throughout, as in continental road races they could not be watched, and walking one day with his wife in the woods below their house, Mr Locke King proposed that they should build it. Prompted neither by yearning for publicity nor the craze for novelty, he desired merely to win, and regain for England the hegemony of the world in this new sport, new science, new industry, foreseeing there the shadow of a great future. Popular apathy to motor-racing made it an astonishingly brave, a very hazardous adventure, complicated by the absence of any other track like that desired or data or experience for a foundation; they supposed with ignorance, laughable now but then only natural, that the track would be quite flat, not wider than twenty feet, suited to a maximum of sixty miles an hour. Indeed, the great Levassor said that anyone who attempted over sixty was a lunatic as well as a criminal. But when they gave the business of design to Colonel Holden, who designed the first motor bicycle, a man interested in cars since 1895, and the very first Chairman of the

Competitions Committee of the R.A.C., he pointed out that banking would be essential; and on this subject there were some curious views revealed, his estimate of twenty-eight feet being first read as twenty-eight inches, and from another quarter coming the theory that it was indeed essential to bank, but on a convex rather than concave curve. The wild compost of freak and folly and abortion that Brooklands might have been enhances the merit of what it is, a show of engineering conspicuously ahead of its time, not yet after a progressive quarter-century outmoded.

Colonel Holden went to Weybridge, saw the acres of wood and pond over which the track would have to be constructed, reconciled Mr Locke King to the stated height of banking, and in autumn 1906 all contracts were signed, all arrangements ready for a start. The trees, the water, the bluebells, were to go and in their place be built a circuit almost three miles long, oval-shaped, with two banked curves set at radii of 1,000 and 1,500 feet, a Finishing Straight of one kilometre, and the whole – this was resolved on later – to be made of concrete; besides there should be grandstands for thirty thousand people, if they came, and the name be the Brooklands Racing Course, after its owner's house that overlooks it.

A.P.Bradley & Michael Burn, Wheels Take Wings *(c.1932)*.

Golfing in Surrey

Who will deny that Surrey occupies a pre-eminent position among golfing counties – and in what county is the 'royal and ancient' game not played to-day? – when it is borne in mind that the Royal Blackheath Golf Club had its beginning so far back as 1608? That is the oldest club in Surrey *[although it is now no longer within the county boundary]*. Next in order of seniority comes the London Scottish, inaugurated in 1866, with a course on Wimbledon Common, followed two years later by the Royal Wimbledon Golf Club. In those early days of the game in England, the vast majority of the players were Scotsmen, who relieved their homesickness with the manipulation of the niblick and the driving iron, while the average Englishman, not comprehending the plan of the game, looked upon it (to use a Scottish phrase) as something uncanny. The game cannot be said to have made rapid progress in Surrey, for until 1885 there appear to have been but four clubs in the whole county, viz., the Royal Blackheath, the London Scottish, the Royal Wimbledon, and the Clapham Common.

But even when golf began to attract a few players, it was looked at askance by the general public, and a lot of pressure was put on the responsible authorities to prevent the game being played on open ground, on the plea that it was highly dangerous to passers by. As the outcome of this opposition, in Surrey a bye-law was enacted, directing that golf players should be attended by a 'fore caddie,' *i.e.*, a man with a red flag walking in front of the player in the same direction as the ball was supposed *(sic)* to go! No wonder this bye-law was unsatisfactory, alike to player and non-player! At any rate, the final outcome of the matter was that on most of the commons near London, play was permitted only during specified hours in the morning or on certain days. But the golfer is not to be denied; these limitations proved far too irksome; and taking other things into consideration, golfers have gradually removed their venue farther away from London.

W.E. Hitchin, Surrey at the Opening of the 20th Century *(1906)*.

Shrove Tuesday Football in Dorking *(1878)*

The doings on Shrove Tuesday in Dorking were quite as lively fifty years ago as at present. In the morning of the day the footballs were carried round the town in the same way as they are now; there was the same collection, too, for broken windows and other damages during the game. How long this old custom had existed before that time I cannot say. When I first remember the morning procession, it consisted of two or three grotesquely dressed men, one of them as now in female attire, and two or three musicians playing a peculiar air, which from its repetition year after year came to be known as 'the football tune.' Poor 'Bill' Smith, at that time and for many years after, carried the balls, with a gravity of bearing that seemed to indicate the performance of bounden duty. Then there were only two footballs which were usually painted blue, red, black and yellow. The old framework from which the balls were suspended, had not then, as now, the inscription –

>'Kick away, both Whig and Tory,
>Wind and water's Dorking's glory;'

But simply the last line, for the former, though commendable for its liberality, is a modern innovation. It was never explained to me why 'Wind and water are Dorking's glory,' but I have guessed that 'wind' refers to the inflation of the ball, and 'water' to the duckings at one period indulged in. The Hamblins, poor fellows, John, George, and Henry, or as they were commonly known, 'Sailor Jack,' 'Fox,' and 'Chick,' one after the other, for many years, made and mended the balls – the last-named occupation being, at that time, by no means a light one. The game was commenced at the Church gates about the same hour as it is now, and was continued throughout the afternoon. One of the principal tradesmen usually gave the first kick. At that period, it was customary to make one or two bays in West Street, and into these were allowed to flow the blood and refuse from a neighbouring slaughter-house. Into this disgusting fluid the ball was kicked, and the players would go, and the more the latter were besmattered and saturated, the better it was liked. Another objectionable, and even more dangerous practice was then in existence, for in the midst of the game, the cry would be raised, 'The Brook, ' 'The Brook!' and thither the footballers would hasten, and while heated by the sport, would duck each other to their heart's content. It is needless to state that the results of this senseless conduct were most disastrous, for many, of course, caught severe colds, which in the case of one or two young men, who had been previously in the bloom of health, ended in premature death. This deplorable issue had a deterrent effect, and the dangerous practice has now, for many years, been wisely abandoned. Six o'clock was then, as now, the time for closing the game, and punctually, on the arrival of the hour, the sport would cease, and after the players had gathered round the ball as it lay on the ground, and given a hearty hurrah, the pastime was then over for another year.

Charles Rose, Recollections of Old Dorking (1878). The game kicked off at two o'clock in the afternoon. There was no limit to the size of the two teams, which consisted of 'Eastenders' and 'Westenders', the object being to retain the ball in your half of the town until the end of the game. In 1897 it was banned by Surrey County Council, who claimed that it caused an obstruction to the highway, and 52 players were arrested. The following year 60 participants were arrested but thereafter interest in continuing this ancient custom rapidly declined. Perhaps it should be revived!

Three Men in a Boat

The tale of a popular pastime on the Thames which really needs no introduction!

It was while passing through Moulsey Lock that Harris told me about his maze experience. It took us some time to pass through, as we were the only boat, and it is a big lock. I don't think I ever remember to have seen Moulsey Lock, before, with only one boat in it. It is, I suppose, Boulter's not even excepted, the busiest lock on the river.

I have stood and watched it, sometimes, when you could not see any water at all, but only a brilliant tangle of bright blazers and gay caps, and saucy hats, and many-coloured parasols, and silken rugs, and cloaks, and streaming ribbons, and dainty whites; when looking down into the lock from the quay, you might fancy it was a huge box into which flowers of every hue and shade had been thrown pell-mell, and lay piled up in a rainbow heap, that covered every corner.

On a fine Sunday it presents this appearance nearly all day long, while, up the stream, and down the stream, lie, waiting their turn, outside the gates, long lines of still more boats; and boats are drawing near and passing away, so that the sunny river, from the Palace up to Hampton Church, is dotted and decked with yellow, and blue, and orange, and white, and red, and pink. All the inhabitants of Hampton and Moulsey dress themselves up in boating costume, and come and mooch round the lock with their dogs, and flirt, and smoke, and watch the boats; and, altogether, what with the caps and jackets of the men, the pretty coloured dresses of the women, the excited dogs, the moving boats, the white sails, the pleasant landscape, and the sparkling water, it is one of the gayest sights I know of near this dull old London town.

Jerome K. Jerome, Three Men in a Boat (To Say Nothing of the Dog) *(1889).*

13 · CRIME AND PUNISHMENT

The Imaginative Financier of Croydon

The modern side of all these things is best exemplified by the beautiful Town Hall which Croydon has provided for itself, in place of the ugly old building, demolished in 1893. It is a noble building, and stands on a site worthy of it, with broad approaches that permit good views, without which the best of buildings is designed in vain. It marks the starting point of the history of modern Croydon, and is a far cry from the old building of the bygone Local Board days, when the traffic of the High Street was regulated – or supposed to be regulated – by the beadle, and the rates were low, and Croydon was a country town, and everything was dull and humdrum. It was a little unfortunate that the first Mayor of Croydon and Member of Parliament for Tamworth, that highly imaginative financier Jabez Spencer Balfour, should have been wanted by the police, a fugitive from justice brought back from the Argentine, and a criminal convicted of fraud as a company promoter; but accidents will happen, and the Town Council did its best, by turning his portrait face to the wall, and by subsequently (as it is reported) losing it. He was sent in 1895, a little belatedly, to fourteen years' penal servitude, and the victims of his 'Liberator' frauds went into the workhouse for the most part, or died. When he ceases to be V 460 and becomes again Jabez Spencer Balfour what a different world it will seem!

Charles G. Harper, The Brighton Road *(1906).*

Wisteria Lodge

It was nearly six o'clock before we found ourselves in the pretty Surrey village of Esher, with Inspector Baynes as our companion.

Holmes and I had taken things for the night, and found comfortable quarters at the Bull. Finally we set out in the company of the detective on our visit to Wisteria Lodge. It was a cold, dark March evening, with a sharp wind and a fine rain beating upon our faces, a fit setting for the wild common over which our road passed and the tragic goal to which it led us.

A cold and melancholy walk of a couple of miles brought us to a high wooden gate, which opened into a gloomy avenue of chestnuts. The curved and shadowed drive led us to a low, dark house, pitch-black against a slate-coloured sky. From the front window upon the left of the door there peeped a glimmer of a feeble light.

'There's a constable in possession,' said Baynes. 'I'll knock at the window.' He stepped across the grass plot and tapped with his hand on the pane. Through the fogged glass I dimly saw a man spring up from a chair beside the fire, and heard a sharp cry from within the room. An instant later a white-faced, hard-breathing policeman had opened the door, the candle wavering in his trembling hand.

'What's the matter, Walters?' asked Baynes, sharply.

The man mopped his forehead with his handkerchief and gave a long sigh of relief.

'I am glad you have come, sir. It has been a long evening and I don't think my nerve is as good as it was.'

'Your nerve, Walters? I should not have thought you had a nerve in your body.'

'Well, sir, it's this lonely, silent house and the queer thing in the kitchen. Then when you tapped at the window I thought it had come again.'

'That what had come again?'

'The devil, sir, for all I know. It was at the window.'

'What was at the window, and when?'

'It was just about two hours ago. The light was just fading. I was sitting reading in the chair. I don't know what made me look up, but there was a face looking in at me through the lower pane. Lord, sir, what a face it was! I'll see it in my dreams.'

'Tut, tut, Walters! This is not talk for a police-constable.'

'I know, sir, I know; but it shook me, sir, and there's no use to deny it. It wasn't black, sir, nor was it white, nor any colour that I know, but a kind of queer shade like clay with a splash of milk in it. Then there was the size of it – it was twice yours, sir. And the look of it – the great staring goggle eyes, and the line of white teeth like a hungry beast. I tell you, sir, I couldn't move a finger, nor get my breath, till it whisked away and was gone. Out I ran and through the shrubbery, but thank God there was no one there.'

'If I didn't know you were a good man, Walters, I should put a black mark against you for this. If it were the devil himself a constable on duty should never thank God that he could not lay his hands upon him. I suppose the whole thing is not a vision and a touch of nerves?'

'That, at least, is very easily settled,' said Holmes, lighting his little pocket lantern. 'Yes,' he reported, after a short examination of the grass bed, 'a number twelve shoe, I should say. If he was all on the same scale as his foot he must certainly have been a giant.'

'What became of him?'

'He seems to have broken through the shrubbery and made for the road.'

'Well,' said the inspector, with a grave and thoughtful face, 'whoever he may have been, and whatever he may have wanted, he's gone for the present, and we have more immediate things to attend to. Now, Mr. Holmes, with your permission, I will show you round the house.'

The various bedrooms and sitting-rooms had yielded nothing to a careful search. Apparently the tenants had brought little or nothing with them, and all the furniture down to the smallest details had been taken over with the house. A good deal of clothing with the stamp of Marx & Co., High Holborn, had been left behind. Telegraphic inquiries had been already made which showed that Marx knew nothing of his customer save that he was a good payer. Odds and ends, some pipes, a few novels, two of them in Spanish, an old-fashioned pinfire revolver, and a guitar were amongst the personal property.

'Nothing in all this, ' said Baynes, stalking, candle in hand, from room to room. 'But now, Mr. Holmes, I invite your attention to the kitchen.'

It was a gloomy, high-ceilinged room at the back of the house, with a straw litter in one corner, which served apparently as a bed for the cook. The table was piled with half-eaten dishes and dirty plates, the debris of last night's dinner.

'Look at this,' said Baynes. 'What do you make of it?'

He held up his candle before an extraordinary object which stood at the back of the dresser. It was so wrinkled and shrunken and withered that it was difficult to say what it might have been. One could but say that it was black and leathery and that it bore some resemblance to a dwarfish human figure. At first, as I examined it, I thought that it was a mummified negro baby, and then it seemed a very twisted and ancient monkey. Finally I was left in doubt as to whether it was animal or human. A double band of white shells was strung round the centre of it.

'Very interesting – very interesting indeed!' said Holmes peering at this sinister relic. 'Anything more?'

In silence Baynes led the way to the sink and held forward his candle. The limbs and body of some large white bird, torn savagely to pieces with the feathers still on, were littered all over it. Holmes pointed to the wattles on the severed head.

'A white cock,' said he; 'most interesting! It is really a very curious case.'

But Mr. Baynes had kept his most sinister exhibit to the last. From under the sink he drew a zinc pail which contained a quantity of blood. Then from the table he took a platter heaped with small pieces of charred bone.

'Something has been killed and something has been burned. We raked all these out of the fire. We had a doctor in this morning. He says that they are not human.'

Holmes smiled and rubbed his hands.

'I must congratulate you, inspector, on handling so distinctive and instructive a case. Your powers, if I may say so without offence, seem superior to your opportunities.'

Inspector Baynes' small eyes twinkled with pleasure.

'You're right, Mr. Holmes. We stagnate in the provinces. A case of this sort gives a man a chance, and I hope that I shall take it. What do you make of these bones?'

'A lamb, I should say, or a kid.'

'And the white cock?'

'Curious, Mr Baynes, very curious. I should say almost unique.'

'Yes, sir, there must have been some very strange people with some very strange ways in this house. One of them is dead. Did his companions follow him and kill him? If they did we should have them, for every port is watched. But my own views are different. Yes, sir, my own views are very different.'

'You have a theory, then?'

'And I'll work it myself Mr. Holmes. It's only due to my own credit to do so. Your name is made, but I have still to make mine. I should be glad to be able to say afterwards that I had solved it without your help.'

Holmes laughed good-humouredly.

'Well, well, inspector,' said he. 'Do you follow your path and I will follow mine. My results are always very much at your service if you care to apply to me for them. I think that I have seen all that I wish in this house, and that my time may be more profitably employed elsewhere. *Au revoir* and good luck!'

Sir Arthur Conan Doyle, His Last Bow *(1917)*.

Lawless Esher

. . . we proceeded to the 'West end,' – a most marshy, stinking, and choleraic locality, compelling me to be continually sniffing at my camphor, and, doubtless, impressing the inhabitants with the notion that I was a gentlemen with a disease in my nose, who was taking precautions to prevent the loss of that member – the losing of which, as Lord Chesterfield told his son, had nothing of the romantic in it – to get a view of the house where the terrible murder had been committed a few months previously. Our morbid curiosity was fully gratified, and we were returning amid 'the odour and harmony of eve,' when there appeared approaching us in the distance what seemed to be a 'fashionable old buck,' who, on a nearer approach, proved to be a fine, tall, portly man of about fifty, beautifully attired in blue trowsers, patent boots, blue coat with brass buttons, white waistcoat, white tie, nobby hat and umbrella, and shirt with a frill. Seeing all this in a second with our wonted minuteness of observation, we prepared ourselves to make passing comment on the weather, and to wish the elegant stranger a 'Bon jour, Monsieur,' when we were considerably startled by his inquiring whether we could 'give a poor man a penny;' and on stating our readiness and ability to assist suffering humanity to that amount, provided a deserving applicant were to produce himself, by his avowing with the greatest coolness that *he* was the deserving party in question. Not being able 'to see that' satisfactorily, we announced the intention of self and coin to be longer acquainted, and passed on, leaving our begging Brummel swearing most inelegantly.

On inquiry, we learnt that Esher was generally infested by tramps and thieves, it being just about without the limits of some Vagrant Act; and that, lying moreover on the high-road to Portsmouth, the discharged prisoners from the gaol at Kingston always made it their first headquarters, and regularly begged it through, to get their hand in again.

Charming place as Esher undeniably is, I don't think, if I had a family of young children extensively got up, and a grand collection of family and modern plate, I should like to rent a mansion in the neighbourhood.

M.C. *Turner,* A Saunter Through Surrey *(1857).*

Coldharbour Cricketers and Smugglers

Coldharbour is really an indentation hammered out of the precipitous flank of Leith Hill, giving room on which to build a little village, a church, and a cricket ground where fielders are always kept busy. From the bedroom windows of the row of little cottages overlooking the cricket ground, and gazing between the tops of the trees of the woods below, curved like a swallow in flight, you look across the blue Weald to the South Downs. So fine is the view here, so bracing the air and free the ground to roam over, that those who wish to obtain lodgings at Coldharbour in the summer have to write for them many weeks, or even months, beforehand.

In one of these cottages lived a young man whose acquaintance I made on the cricket pitch. It was between the innings, when, fatigued with his fast-bowling delivery, he lay upon his back and began discussing Nietzsche, that we first became friends. We were a motley team – coachmen, gardeners, gamekeepers, labourers, tradesmen, 'gentlemen' – such as usually make up the membership of a country cricket club. A little green patch of cricket ground is the only oasis in the desert of snobbery where classes are for a brief moment forgotten in rural England.

My clever young friend had to endure much from the stultifying mental atmosphere that surrounded him. He took to tramping through the country, visiting Parisian ateliers, writing art criticisms and short stories, and the last I heard of him was that he was finishing a novel at Hyères.

It must have been of this district of Coldharbour, which was an old smuggling centre, that Miss Jekyll relates an amusing story.

'When the country people discovered the hiding-place of the contraband goods, the result of a successful 'run,' it was customary for the finder to put a chalk mark on a small proportion of the number of articles. When the smugglers went again to collect their kegs, the marked ones were left. This was well understood as a bargain, in consideration of the discovery not being reported.

'A squire, new to the country, came to live at a place in the hills near Dorking in the early part of the nineteenth century. One morning, before he was dressed, his valet brought him an urgent message from the bailiff to say that he wished to see him. The master said he must wait, as he was not dressed. The message came again, still more pressingly worded.

"Well, send the fellow up," said the unfinished squire.

'The man came in with a mysterious air and watched the servant out of the room, and then said in a hoarse half-whisper: "There was a run last night, sir, and I have marked four."

'The squire had not the least idea what the information meant, and on being enlightened he burst out indignantly: "But I can't have anything to do with smuggled goods; why, I am a magistrate. How dare you come to me with such a suggestion!"

'The bailiff stood his ground quite unabashed. "If you'll take my word for it, sir, if you don't do as others do, you'll have trouble."

'The squire continuing to protest vigorously, the bailiff said: "Well, sir, will you ask the parson?"

'He did so, and the rector's answer was: "If you wish to live in peace with your neighbours, you had better fall in with the custom of the country."' A very old man told Professor Malden how he as a child remembered his father holding open a gate at the end of Crocker's Lane, Coldharbour, that thirty men on horseback with kegs of brandy behind them might ride through – a picture which brings Mr. Kipling's ringing ballad to one's mind:

> 'If you meet King George's men, dressed in blue and red,
> You be careful what you say, and mindful what is said.
> If they call you 'pretty maid' and chuck you 'neath the chin,
> Don't you tell where no one is, nor yet where no one's been.
> If you do as you've been told, likely there's a chance,
> You'll be given a dainty doll, all the way from France,
> With a cap of Valenciennes, and a velvet hood –
> A present from the Gentlemen, along o' being good!
>   Five and twenty ponies
>   Trotting through the dark –
>   Brandy for the Parson,
>   'Baccy for the Clerk.
> Them that asks no questions isn't told a lie –
> Watch the wall, my darling, while the Gentlemen go by!'

F.E. Green, The Surrey Hills (1915).

The Flying Highwayman

The Flying Highwayman, on Monday last, robbed the Derby Machine. A young Lady gave him a green Purse, in which were eight Counters and two Shillings, with which he seemed well pleased.

The same Highwayman called at a House near Godstone in Surry, where he ordered a roast Fowl for his Supper; and was just going to pull off his Boots, when a travelling Man came in with a Box of Lace, and called for sixpenny worth of Rum and Water, which the Highwayman partook of, and then he called for another in Return; during the drinking of it, the Laceman declared himself how far he was going that Night, which was but a few Miles off, and took his leave presently. Afterwards the Highwayman called the Ostler, to know if he had watered his Horse, and was answered in the

Affirmative, on which he ordered him to give him some more; when he came back, he fell aswearing that he had then given him too much and said the Horse was cold, and all of a Tremble; on which he put the Bridge and Saddle on and said he would ride him up and down the Road to warm him while the Fowl was roasting. Accordingly away he went after the Laceman, whom he robbed of twenty Pounds and his Box of Lace, charging him not to come back at his Peril; and then rode back to the Inn, and bidding the Landlord give him his Gloves and Whip, he had left on the Table, told him he had altered his Mind, and left five Shillings for the Fowl and sixpenny worth of Rum and Water, and made off. In about a Quarter of an Hour after the Laceman came back, with two Farmers Men, hue and cry, but the Bird was flown.

Cutting from an unidentified newspaper dated 1761.

The Unknown Sailor

The following can still be read on the gravestone of a sailor in Thursley churchyard, 'who was barbarously murdered on Hindhead' on 24th September, 1786.

> When pitying Eyes to see my Grave shall come,
> And with a generous Tear bedew my Tomb;
> Here shall they read my melancholy Fate,
> With Murder and Barbarity complete.
> In perfect Health and in the Flow'r of Age,
> I fell a Victim to three Ruffians' Rage:
> On bended Knees I mercy strove t'obtain,
> Their Thirst of Blood made all Entreaties vain.
> No dear Relation; or still dearer Friend,
> Weeps my Hard Lot, or Miserable End;
> Yet o'er my sad Remains (my Name unknown)
> A generous Public have inscribed this Stone.

A Burglary Near Chertsey

It was now intensely dark. The fog was much heavier than it had been in the early part of the night; and the atmosphere was so damp, that, although no rain fell, Oliver's hair and eyebrows, within a few minutes after leaving the house, had become stiff with the half-frozen moisture that was floating about. They crossed the bridge; and kept on towards the lights which he had seen before. They were at no great distance off; and, as they walked pretty briskly, they soon arrived at Chertsey.

'Slap through the town,' whispered Sikes; 'there'll be nobody in the way, to-night, to see us.'

Toby acquiesced; and they hurried through the main street of the little town, which at that late hour was wholly deserted. A dim light shone at intervals from some bed-room window; and the hoarse barking of dogs occasionally broke the silence of the night. But there was nobody abroad; and they cleared the town, as the church-bell struck two.

Quickening their pace, they turned up a road upon the left hand. After walking about a quarter of a mile, they stopped before a detached house surrounded by a wall: to the top of which, Toby Crackit, scarcely pausing to take breath, climbed in a twinkling.

'The boy next,' said Toby. 'Hoist him up; I'll catch hold of him.'

Before Oliver had time to look round, Sikes had caught him under the arms; and in three or four seconds he and Toby were lying on the grass on the other side. Sikes followed directly. And they stole cautiously towards the house.

And now, for the first time, Oliver, well nigh mad with grief and terror, saw that housebreaking and robbery, if not murder, were the objects of the expedition. He clasped his hands together, and involuntarily uttered a subdued exclamation of horror. A mist came before his eyes; the cold sweat stood upon his ashy face; his limbs failed him; and he sunk upon his knees.

'Get up!' murmured Sikes, trembling with rage, and drawing the pistol from his pocket. 'Get up, or I'll strew your brains upon the grass.'

'Oh! For God's sake let me go!' cried Oliver; 'let me run away and die in the fields. I will never come near London; never, never! Oh! Pray have mercy on me, and do not make me steal. For the love of all the bright Angels that rest in Heaven, have mercy upon me!'

The man to whom this appeal was made, swore a dreadful oath, and had cocked the pistol, when Toby, striking it from his grasp, placed his hand upon the boy's mouth, and dragged him to the house.

'Hush!' cried the man; 'it won't answer here. Say another word, and I'll do your business myself with a crack on the head. That makes no noise; and is quite as certain, and more genteel. Here, Bill, wrench the shutter open. He's game enough now, I'll engage. I've seen older hands of his age took the same way, for a minute or two, on a cold night.'

Sikes, invoking terrific imprecations upon Fagin's head for sending Oliver on such an errand, plied the crowbar vigorously, but with little noise. After some delay, and some assistance from Toby, the shutter to which he had referred, swung open on its hinges.

It was a little lattice window, about five feet and a half above the ground: at the back of the house: which belonged to the scullery, or small brewing-place, at the end of the passage. The aperture was so small, that the inmates had probably not thought it worth while to defend it more securely; but it was large enough to admit a boy of Oliver's size, nevertheless. A very brief exercise of Mr Sikes's art, sufficed to overcome the fastening of the lattice; and it soon stood wide open also.

'Now listen, you young limb,' whispered Sikes, drawing a dark lattern from his pocket, and throwing the glare full on Oliver's face; 'I'm a going to put you through there. Take this light; go softly up the steps straight afore you; and along the little hall to the street-door; unfasten it, and let us in.'

'There's a bolt at the top, you won't be able to reach,' interposed Toby. 'Stand upon one of the hall chairs. There are three there, Bill, with a jolly large blue unicorn and a gold pitchfork on 'em: which is the old lady's arms.'

'Keep quiet, can't you?' replied Sikes, with a threatening look. 'The room-door is open, is it?'

'Wide,' replied Toby, after peeping in to satisfy himself. 'The game of that, is, that they always leave it open with a catch, so that the dog, who's got a bed in here, may walk up and down the passage when he feels wakeful. Ha! Ha! Barney 'ticed him away to-night. So neat!'

Although Mr. Crackit spoke in a scarcely audible whisper, and laughed without noise, Sikes imperiously commanded him to be silent, and get to work. Toby complied, by first producing his lantern, and placing it on the ground; and then by planting himself firmly with his head against the wall beneath the window, and his hands upon his knees, so as to make a step of his back. This was no sooner done, than Sikes, mounting upon him, put Oliver gently through the window with his feet first; and, without leaving hold of his collar, planted him safely on the floor inside.

'Take this lantern,' said Sikes, looking into the room. 'You see the stairs afore you?'

Oliver, more dead than alive, gasped out 'Yes.' Sikes pointing to the street-door with the pistol-barrel, briefly advised him to take notice that he was within shot all the way; and that if he faltered, he would fall dead that instant.

'It's done in a minute,' said Sikes, in the same low whisper. 'Directly I leave go of you, do your work. Hark!'

'What's that?' whispered the other man.

They listened intently.

'Nothing,' said Sikes, releasing his hold of Oliver. 'Now!'

In the short time he had had to collect his senses, the boy had firmly resolved that, whether he died in the attempt or not, he would make one effort to dart upstairs from the hall, and alarm the family. Filled with this idea, he advanced at once, but stealthily.

'Come back!' suddenly cried Sikes aloud. 'Back! back!'

The cry was repeated – a light appeared – a vision of two terrified half-dressed men at the top of the stairs swam before his eyes – a flash – a loud noise – a smoke – a crash somewhere, but where he knew not, – and he staggered back.

Sikes had disappeared for an instant; but he was up again, and had him by the collar before the smoke had cleared away.

He fired his own pistol after the men, who were already retreating; and dragged the boy up.

'Clasp your arm tighter,' said Sikes, as he drew him through the window. 'Give me a shawl here. They've hit him. Quick! Damnation, how the boy bleeds!'

Then came the loud ringing of a bell: mingled with the noise of fire-arms, and the shouts of men, and the sensation of being carried over uneven ground at a rapid pace. And then, the noises grew confused in the distance; and a cold deadly feeling crept over the boy's heart; and he saw or heard no more.

Charles Dickens, Oliver Twist *(1838)*.

The Lingfield Cage

Lingfield is not large enough, nor enough overbuilt and railway-ridden, to dare to the title of capital even of a distant corner of Surrey. But it stands above and apart from the quiet country round it, like a Bible in an old library. Near it, or in its streets, are some of the prettiest and most ancient timber houses in the county; the churchyard with its brick paths, its rose-beds, the red walls round it and its view of the Weald, has the serenity of deep meadowland and sunlit cloisters; the church itself, with its ancient carved oak and baronial tombs, belongs to all English history from Creçy. If the churches of the surrounding parishes, with their brasses and their registers, make up an admirable local guide-book, the records of Lingfield church are a chapter of Hume.

The village itself is the pleasantest mixture of every style of Surrey cottage, brick and timber, weather-tiling, plain brick, plain wood, and a queer row of square white-stuccoed buildings which looks as if it had been dumped inland from opposite shingle and dancing seas. It lacks tamarisk to be sheer Worthing. The village centres on its pond; not a broad or very limpid piece of water, but distinguished by a pair of swans, and by a curious obelisk standing at its head which once marked a shrine. Built on to the bole of an old oak by the obelisk is an apartment engagingly labelled 'Ye Village Cage.' Other Surrey villages have had their cages, but only Lingfield has kept one. The door is massive and threatening, and you get the keys at the chemist's the other side of the road; or rather, a guide politely accompanies you and displays the cage's secrets. The cage not long ago fell into disuse. It was once used as a temporary lock-up for drunk or disorderly persons, or others who had traversed the local by-laws of morality. Local justices descended upon them, and they were cast into durance until morning should bring soberness with a headache, or, in more serious cases, until proper conveyance could be got round for Godstone. The cage has seen at least one exciting rescue. This was some fifty or sixty years ago, when a number of desperate characters vaguely described as the Copthorne poachers were captured and haled into prison. As to the exact number of captives, tradition varies; but the legend which is the most respectful to the powers of the local constable sets it at eleven. The eleven were surrounded, the door of the dungeon closed on them, and the village tried to go to sleep. Darkness came on, and a daring deed. Other poachers stole into the village, got to work with picks and crowbars, took the roof off the dungeon and hauled out their comrades exulting. The village wisely did not attempt a recapture.

The cage saw its last tenant in 1882, and the story of the rescued poachers could for long be heard from the mouth of the oldest inhabitant, who was himself at one time a constable. As an expert in suppressing crime, he never liked the plan on which the cage was built. The floor is higher by two steps than the ground outside, and you had to go upstairs to it. In fact, you had to throw your prisoner upstairs – a most perilous business. It ought to have been built so that you could take him by the left leg and throw him downstairs like a Christian.

Caged prisoners at Lingfield were not always treated with the utmost rigour of the law. At one time the door was pierced by a grating, and through the grating kindly souls passed packets of tobacco. Liquor could not be passed in packets, but found its way in somehow. Afterwards in severer days the grating was closed, the prisoners neither drank nor smoked, as became their miserable condition. Nine years after the last captive languished behind the blocked grating the prison was taken over by the village for fresh purposes. Henceforward it was to be the museum, and was duly vested in trustees. Its collection still grows slowly. 'Anything to do with village crime – we make that our special subject,' the curator informs you with a pleasing urbaneness. The collection includes a man-trap, a pair of handcuffs, a canvas bed which furnishes the museum whenever it is wanted as a mortuary, a pair of farmer's snowboots used a hundred years ago, and a pair of farmer's ordinary boots used more recently.

Eric Parker, Highways and Byways in Surrey, *2nd edition (1935). A lock-up also survives intact at Ewell.*

15 · AT WAR

The Battle of Dorking

In 1871 an article appeared in Blackwood's Magazine *under the pseudonym, 'A Volunteer', which retold the story of the supposed German invasion of England following the defeat of France in 1870. The author was Sir George Chesney, who had served in the Indian Army and had been badly wounded in the Indian Mutiny in 1857. The story caused quite a stir at the time and was republished in booklet form which ran to many editions.*

You ask me to tell you, my grandchildren, something about my own share in the great events that happened fifty years ago. 'Tis sad work turning back to that bitter page in our history, but you may perhaps take profit in your new homes from the lesson it teaches. For us in England it came too late . . .

It was on a Monday that the declaration of war was announced, and in a few hours we got our first inkling of the sort of preparation the enemy had made for the event which they had really brought about, although the actual declaration was made by us. A pious appeal to the God of battles, whom it was said we had aroused, was telegraphed back; and from that moment all communication with the north of Europe was cut off . . .

At the first sign of dawn the bugles of the regiments sounded the

reveillé, and we were ordered to fall in, and roll was called. About twenty men were absent, who had fallen out sick the day before; they had been sent up to London by train during the night, I believe. After standing in column for about half an hour, the brigade-major came down with orders to pile arms and stand easy; and perhaps half an hour afterwards we were told to get breakfast as quickly as possible, and to cook a day's food at the same time . . . Meantime there was leisure to look around, and from where we stood there was a commanding view of one of the most beautiful scenes in England. Our regiment was drawn up on the extremity of the ridge which runs from Guildford to Dorking. This is indeed merely a part of the great chalk-range which extends from beyond Aldershot east to the Medway; but there is a gap in the ridge just here where a little stream that runs past Dorking turns suddenly to the north, to find its way to the Thames.
. . . Anybody, indeed, might have been struck with the natural advantages of our position; but what, I remember, most impressed me, was the peaceful beauty of the scene – the little town with the outline of the houses obscured by a blue mist, the massive crispness of the foliage, the outlines of the great trees, lighted up by the sun, and relieved by deep-blue shade . . .

The officers told us that the enemy's advanced-guard was close behind, but that he had apparently been waiting for reinforcements, and would probably not attack in force until noon. It was, however, nearly three o'clock before the battle began. We had almost worn out the feeling expectancy. For twelve hours had we been waiting for the coming struggle, till at last it seemed almost as if the invasion were but a bad dream, and the enemy, as yet unseen by us, had no real existence. So far things had not been very different, but for the numbers and for what we had been told, from a Volunteer review on Brighton Downs. I remember that these thoughts were passing through my mind as we lay down in groups on the grass, some smoking, some nibbling at their bread, some even asleep, when the listless state we had fallen into was suddenly disturbed by a gunshot fired from the top of the hill on our right, close by the big house . . . This gun was apparently the signal to begin, for now our batteries opened fire all along the line . . .

And now the enemy's artillery began to open; where their guns were posted we could not see, but we began to hear the rush of the shells over our heads, and the bang as they burst just beyond. And now what took place I can really hardly tell you . . .

Our colonel and major must have been shot, for there was no one to give an order, when somebody on horseback called from behind – I think it must have been the brigadier – 'Now, then, volunteers! Give a British cheer, and go at them – charge!' and, with a shout, we rushed at the enemy. Some of them ran, some stopped to meet us, and for a moment it was a real hand-to-hand fight. I felt a sharp sting in my leg, as I drove my bayonet right through the man in front of me. I confess I shut my eyes, for I just got a glimpse of the poor wretch as he fell back, his eyes starting out of his head, and, savage though we were, the sight was almost too horrible to look at. But the struggle was over in a second, and we had cleared the ground again right up to the rear hedge of the lane. Had we gone on, I believe we might have recovered the lane too, but we were now all out of order; there was no one to say what to do; the enemy began to line the hedge and open fire, and they were streaming past our left; and how it came about I know not, but we found ourselves falling back towards our right rear, scarce any semblance of a line remaining, and the volunteers who had given way on our left mixed up with us, and added to the confusion. It was now nearly dark . . .

This halt first gave us time to think about what had happened. The long day of expectancy had been succeeded by the excitement of battle; and when each minute may be your last, you do not think much about other people, nor when you are facing another man with a rifle have you time to consider whether he or you are the invader, or that you are fighting for your home and hearths. All fighting is pretty much alike, I suspect, as to sentiment, when once it begins. But now we had time for reflection; and although we did not yet quite understand how far the day had gone against us, an uneasy feeling of self-condemnation must have come up in the minds of most of us; while, above all, we now began to realise what the loss of this battle meant to the country . . .

Happy those whose bones whitened the fields of Surrey; they at least were spared the disgrace we lived to endure. Even you, who have never known what it is to live otherwise than on sufferance, even your cheeks burn when we talk of these days; think, then, what those endured who, like your grandfather, had been citizens of the proudest nation on earth . . . Truly the nation was ripe for a fall; but when I reflect how a little firmness and self-denial, or political courage and foresight, might have averted the disaster, I feel that the judgement must have really been deserved. A nation too selfish to defend its liberty, could not have been fit to retain it. To you, my grandchildren, who are now going to seek a new home in a more prosperous land, let not this bitter lesson be lost upon you in the country of your adoption. For me, I am too old to begin life again in a strange country; and hard and evil as have been my days, it is not much to await in solitude the time which cannot now be far off, when my old bones will be laid to rest in the soil I have loved so well, and whose happiness and honour I have so long survived.

The Battle of Dorking: *Reminiscences of a Volunteer (1871)*.

A Memory of the Great War

My parents moved to Surrey when I was six. We had one of a block of twelve houses, the only houses then in Wallington, between South Beddington and Waddon. Croydon Aerodrome was only a couple of fields away.

Years later, when war broke out, Croydon Aerodrome was a training centre for the Royal Flying Corps. I woke one Sunday morning and a plane was coming straight for my bedroom window. Fortunately we had a very high wooden swing at the end of the garden and the left wing tip just caught this and swung round. The plane ending up nose down in our potato patch. I went into my parents' bedroom and told them. 'Oh yes, dear! We know it's April Fool's Day', which indeed it was. The noise of hundreds of people swarming in our garden convinced them something was up.

How so many people could appear from nowhere at seven o'clock in the morning was beyond us. They stripped that plane to its bones. The Adjutant was furious, it was a new one and had only been flying six hours. The pilot – a Captain Berry – was doing his sixth solo flight. He only broke his nose on the joystick but was grounded for six months, this being their lot if they pranged on the sixth flight. We couldn't grow anything in the kitchen garden for years. My brother, confined to bed with mumps, was given the propeller – the Adjutant said there was no use keeping it, the public hadn't left much else. The brand new plane was a write-of at a cost of £1,000 plus, a lot of money in those days.

Surrey Federation of Women's Institutes, Surrey Within Living Memory *(1992)*.

Little Girl Talked Cheerfully and then She Died

The village of Brockham, beneath the Downs and just a few miles from Dorking had been slightly bombed and machine-gunned and some villagers had seen a Canadian soldier open fire on a German parachutist as he baled out of his crashing plane.

On October 4th [1940] the village was rocked by tragedy when bombs fell on Nutwood Avenue and five were killed. In one house were Mrs Daisy Herrington, her daughter June and George Biggs an evacuee. Next door, Mrs Esther Fisher and her two-year-old son William died.

A rescue party worked frantically and courageously through the night and among them was Edith Mercer, a volunteer member of the Dorking General Hospital Mobile First Aid Unit. Here is an extract from her wartime diary which related to that incident.

'At 12.30 when I was falling asleep, a summons – to Brockham. Four of us went in Mrs Kaye's car and she seemed to have great difficulty in driving and seeing even though the searchlights were providing quite a lot of illumination. We lost our way and were redirected. We eventually arrived at Nutwood Avenue, where two houses, little semi-detached ones, had been razed by a couple of high explosive shells. One could just see the outlines in the dark and the rescue party scrambling among the rubbish with torches.

Someone, a neighbour, was giving an account of the people in the houses. Two had apparently been taken out already with not too serious injuries.

There were others underneath, a baby, two women, an evacuee boy and a little girl of seven. Dr Bourn-Taylor evidently decided there were enough people in attendance and, without authority, I imagine, ordered the mobile unit back to Dorking. We were hardly back, when we were summoned again to the same place, where we stayed for the rest of the night.

It was a nightmarish unreal sort of scene, the dimly seen collapsed houses, without a wall standing. The rescue party with torches among the ruins, the rest, about 20 people standing in the road waiting to be of assistance, the searchlights overhead, the buzz of planes and the distant anti-aircraft fire. Every now and again torches had to be put out completely until the raiders were past. Two bodies were brought out. A little girl of seven was alive but pinned down by the arm and shoulder. She was able to talk quite cheerfully and did not seem too badly injured.

It was towards rescuing her that the efforts of the night were directed. Dr Bourn-Taylor got near enough to talk to her and later we prepared a wad on the end of a stick moistened with warm water or tea which could be passed to her lips. At six o'clock it was light enough to see and most of the Mobile Unit went back to the car. J and I stayed with the doctor and nurses. But it was all no good for about seven o'clock the child became unconscious and died.

People round about were very hospitable with tea and kettles of water. One curious collection of country folk in a kitchen I went into should have been painted. An old fashioned kitchen range, a large cage of birds, a big black dog, assorted large women, crowded furniture, children in grubby pyjamas, a shock-headed boy and a man heating up kettles for us – all at three o'clock in the morning'.

Bob Ogley, Surrey at War 1939-1945 (1995).

The Home Guard

The Home Guard was set up in May 1940 and originally called the Local Defence Volunteers or LDV for short. The 4th (Guildford) Battalion Surrey Home Guard was commanded by Colonel Guy Geddes, an ex-professional soldier, who had retired in 1934. The inspiration for the ever popular television series, 'Dads' Army', is perhaps occasionally obvious here.

John Wakefield and his father joined the LDV in Guildford as soon as it was set up. John was working at Vokes in Normandy [the one near Guildford!] and his father, John senior, was also in a reserved occupation. His was an unusual but important job. He had fought in the First World War and was now a bill poster with his own office in

The Bars off Chertsey Street. One of his jobs was to go around the borough posting Government and other important notices on official boards and church doors. Father and son were attached to A Company, 4th Battalion (Guildford) Surrey Home Guard, whose company commander was H.G. Stafford of Tilehurst Estate.

Their platoon met in an outbuilding of a house called Sudpre at Pitch Place, Worplesdon. There was a small rifle range on which the men could practice and they did manoeuvres and patrols on nearby Whitmoor Common. John recalls that it was great fun to be able to handle their one and only anti-tank rifle complete with its own stand! Most turns of duty began with a visit to the nearby Ship public house before they 'fell in' at Sudpre. Evidently, any late comers who missed their chance for a beer were inclined to be quite grumpy. So the officer in charge often sent them off to the pub for a quick pint knowing that when they returned they would have cheered up a bit!

. . . Finally, on January 2, 1941, the men received their first issue of serge battledress, helmets, haversacks and some more much-needed greatcoats. The following month weapons began to arrive. They included two .300 Vickers machine guns, four Browning medium machine guns and an anti-tank weapon called the Northover Projector. In April 1941 twelve Thompson machine guns were delivered, only to be eventually withdrawn as they were required by the Army instead!

The year ended with the battalions involved in the work of creating anti-tank ditches and road blocks around the perimeter of the borough and being issued with 1,000 rifles and bayonets.

Regular Action Station exercises were to form an important part of the Home Guard's ongoing training. In May 1942, these were held on the 6th, 14th, 16th and 25th. Col. Geddes wrote: 'On the 16th the enemy was represented by a young soldier battalion of the East Surrey Regiment. The clash of arms had its amusing side. The young soldiers, overcome with keenness and excitement, were somewhat contemptuous of the old gentlemen of the Home Guard, and thought that they would be a push over. Their ardour was somewhat dampened by the Home Guard exhibiting a considerable knowledge of unarmed combat, in which a good number had been put through.'

One of that summer's [1943] exercises was for members of E company to pretend to be enemy paratroopers and raid Chilworth railway station 'destroying' the bridge, signal box and sidings, without being challenged by the platoon for that area. E company completed the task with ease. The poor company commander at Chilworth was in the middle of a crossword puzzle when the 'enemy' attacked and before he knew what was happening, the whole drama was over.

Graham Collyer and David Rose, Guildford: the War Years, 1939-45 *(1999)*.

Other Dangers of War

In wartime there were other dangers that threatened those in the process of seeking relief in the privy, as Miss Jordan related: 'In 1940 a German plane dropped a delayed action bomb in our garden at Redhill. It exploded after the 'all clear' had been sounded, along with another one dropped in an adjoining road. Seven houses were destroyed. My mother, having just used the loo, had hold of the door to close it at the exact moment when the bomb exploded. The sizeable yew hedge surrounding the privy saved her from being buried, but she was blown across the yard. All this happened at 11.20 at night.

D.J. Buxton's privy near Send was replaced by a flush loo in 1939 but this strategic improvement soon became a target for the enemy. It was eventually flattened by a flying bomb in 1944.

John Janaway, Surrey Privies *(1999)*.

Bomb Destroys Church

A flying bomb fell on a country church in Southern England just before morning service was due to begin yesterday morning. As the bomb was falling the Rector was on his way to the church. He was not injured. Rescue men, firemen and soldiers searched the rubble in case people had got to church early for the service, but no one was found.

Surrey Advertiser, *August 1944. Because of strict censorship the paper did not disclose the exact location of the bombed church. It was, in fact, Abinger Parish Church.*

15 · AT PARTING

First, a Lesson in Life

The sleepye mynde doth tyme forget
And youthe the toyes doth most desire
Soe tyme once past is hard to get
Too late in adge learnge to acqire

All such as will not labour in tyme
But spend their daies in ydlenesse
Full soone are caught upp in the lyne
Of sorrow payne and wrechednesse

1613

Inscribed on a wooden beam in a house in the High Street of Haslemere and reported by E. W. Swanton in Country Notes *(1938).*

The following was recorded on the gravestone of a carpenter named Spong, who died at Ockham in 1736. Apparently he worked for the King family, whose country seat was at Ockham Park. The 'Hollis' mentioned in the last line was a bricklayer to the same family.

Who many a sturdy oak lain along,
Fell'd by Death's surer hatchet, here lies Spong.
Posts oft he made, yet ne'er a place could get,
And liv'd by railing, tho' he was no wit.
Old saws he had, altho' no Antiquarian;
And styles corrected, yet was no grammarian.
Long liv'd he Ockham's premier architect;
And lasting as his fame a tomb t'erect.
In vain we seek an artist such as he,
Whose pales and gates were for eternity.
So here he rests from all life's toils and follies,
O spare awhile, kind Heav'n, his fellow-labourer Hollis!

Coincidence

Anne the wife of William Wheeler who (as is credibly affirmed) was borne on Octob.18 & was married Octob.18 1625 & died Octob.18 1626, was buried Octob.19.
Newdigate Parish Register

Mum is Barred

In the churchyard at Horsell, Surrey, only full Christian names and surnames – and not abbreviations such as 'Mum' or 'Dad' – are to be allowed on tombstones, the Parochial Church Council has decided. The Decision was made after a letter from a parishioner who quoted this inscription from a tombstone:
'The trumpet sounds, Peter calls 'Come' –
The pearly gates open, and in walks Mum.'
Culled from The Daily Mail, *1st August, 1945.*

Unfortunate Deaths

12 Apl 1641 Ann Vale daughter of Richard, being most miserably burnt to death, was buryed In those parts that the fire had not consumed.

Thomas Dewell buryed 25th of April [1691] who was unfortunately shot to death with his own gun.

Richard Meachim a old man who gat his death by a cart running over him buryed November 9th 1707.
Walton-on-Thames Parish Registers.

Seen on a monument in Warlingham Church:-

> O cruel Death, what hast thou done,
> To take from us our mother's darling son?
> Thou hast taken toll, ground, and drest his grist,
> The brand lieth here, the flour is gone to Christ.

Ockham seems to have been a dangerous place for the artizan, but at least he was guaranteed an unforgetable epitaph:-

> The Lord saw good, I was lopping off wood,
> And down fell from the tree:
> I met with a check, and I broke my neck
> And so death lopped off me.

Epitaph to Thomas Greenhill, who died in 1634 and was buried in Beddington Church:

> Under thy feet interred is here
> A native born in Oxfordshire;
> First, life and learning Oxford gave,
> Surrey, to him, his death and grave.
> He once a Hill was, fresh and green,
> Now, withered, is not to be seen;
> Earth in earth, shovelled up, is shut
> A Hill into a hole is put.

Thomas Humphreys, described as a corpulent barber, who died in September 1742, aged 44, was buried at Carshalton:

> Tom Humphreys lies here, by death
> beguiled,
> Who never did harm to man, woman,
> or child;
> And since without foe no man e'er
> was known,
> Poor Tom was nobody's foe but his
> own.
> Lay light on him earth, for none
> would there be
> (Though heavy his bulk) trip it
> lighter on thee.

1607 Nov. 27 [burial] – John Plonker

1737[1738] January 15 – Henry Smith Junior fell off Busbridge house and spoke one word died.

1739 September 8 – Mr Thomas Gilham and also his wife Buried both in one grave as was also her Mother and Father in Law.
Godalming Parish Registers.

Here is the epitaph to John Rose, who met with an accident at Betchworth:

> Dear friends and companions all,
> Pray take warning from me;
> Don't venture on the ice too far,
> As 'twas the death of me.

Epitaph to George Nye who was buried at Abinger in 1707:

> George Nye was my Name,
> And Ingland was my Nashon;
> Abinger was my Dwelling Plase,
> And Christ is my Salvation.

*The following was recorded by John Aubrey in the late 17th century
on a gravestone in Croydon Parish Church.*

> Curtious Reader knowe that here doth ly
> A rare example of true pietie
> Whose glorie twas to prove herself in life
> A vertuous wooman, and a Loyall wife
> Her name to you obscurely Ille impart
> In this her Anagrame no arme but Hart
> And least you joyne amiss and soe loose the name
> Look underneath & you shall find the same
> Martha Burton the wife of Bernard Burton Esqr
> Deceased the 20th day of November & was buryed
> the 26th day An. Dom. 1668.

Buried with No Name

1614 Feb. 19 – A poare maid was buried. (Godalming)

1642 Nov. 8 – A captain among the cavaleirs, and his boy. (Walton-on-Thames)

1729 July 6 – a strainge child left her name not known. (Godalming)

1772 Sep. 13 – A man who went by the name of one-eyed John. (Compton)

Death of an Aristocrat

*During the mid-18th century the 2nd Duke of Richmond often
stopped overnight at Godalming en route to and from his country seat
at Goodwood in Sussex. On one such trip he was taken ill at Church
House, Godalming.*

8 August 1750

With alternate thrills of hot and cold the Duke lay shivering in a
fever at Godalming. Sedgwick, his secretary, sat anxiously by him.
Wormwood, *Artemisia absinthium*, dark, bitter and oily, was

prescribed to bring down the Duke's temperature. The Duke drank it, hardly aware of his surroundings. He lay between damp sheets, confused by fever and weakened by dehydration. Days and nights passed blurrily in the darkened room. Gradually the house filled up. From London, Truesdale and Middleton, the family doctors, came with medicines and assistants. The Duke's landau brought the Duchess and her servants from Goodwood. Relatives and friends came in and went quietly out. In the midst of this muffled commotion the Duke travelled alone into the dark extinction of death. Slowly but surely fever pulled him into the void from life, light and happiness. On the tenth day the Duke died.

A few hours later Middleton took off his frock-coat and rolled up his fine white cotton sleeves. He picked up his knife, pressed it against the dead Duke's soft, resisting stomach and then pressed harder until the skin broke and parted. Middleton cut a deep, straight line down the Duke's navel. He sliced through the pinky-grey skin, the gelatinous yellow layer of fat and the thick red muscle wall. From the thin skin of the peritoneum Middleton's warm, gloveless hands pulled out the cold intestines and burrowed down into the pelvic cavity to reach the bladder. Picking up a small steel scalpel he slit the bladder open. The bladder was irritated and inflamed like a small balloon but there was no trace of any gall stones.

Left alone in the room to refine and practise his diagnostic skills, Middleton rummaged about amongst the dead Duke's cold and solidifying organs. He split open a section of intestines and examined the stomach. After some time he carefully put the pieces back again, pressing down the grey, sausage-like intestines, and threaded a length of cat gut through the eye of a large needle. He tied a knot in the end of the thread and, pulling the severed skin together, sewed the body up with a line of stitches that ran in parallel down the abdomen. Then he washed his hands in a basin standing on the floor. The Duke's body, cleaned and dressed, was prepared to make its final journey to a dark vault in Chichester Cathedral.

Stella Tillyard, Aristocrats: Caroline, Emily, Louisa and Sarah Lennox 1740-1832 *(1994)*.

More from Ockham Church

The epitaph writers of Ockham showed more skill than the average,
but this rhyme seems to be stretching it a bit!

Here lies the wife of Robert Martin,
She was a good wife to Roger, that's sartin.

Albury

Oh cruel was the man to plant that tree:
The fruit that grew thereon it was the death of me.
Little children, whoever you may be,
Eat not the fruit of the Night-shade tree.
It was sweet unto my taste –
I eat and died – now in the grave I rest.

On the tomb of a child aged two and a half in Albury churchyard.

For Whom the Bell Tolls

The following is inscribed on a bell cast in 1729, one of a peal of six
which hang in the belfry of the Norman tower of Oxted Parish
Church:

Good folks with one accord
we call to hear God's word,
we honour to the king
joy to brides do ring,
we triumphs loudly tell
and ring your last farewell.

ACKNOWLEDGEMENTS

I am grateful to the folowing for allowing the inclusion of both prose and poetry which remains in copyright: Yale University Press for extracts from Ian Nairn & Nikolaus Pevsner's *The Buildings of England: Surrey*; Longmans, Green & Co for pieces from Gertrude Jekyll's *Old West Surrey;* Wordsworth Editions Ltd for an extract from *The Works of Rudyard Kipling*; A & C Black for permission to use Gordon Home's *The Charm of Surrey* 1929; Macmillan, London, U.K. for a piece from Eric Parker's *Highways and Byways in Surrey*; John Murray for extracts from John Betjeman's *Collected Poems*; Countryside Books for pieces from the Surrey Federation of Women's Institutes' *Surrey within Living Memory*; David Higham Associates for the paragraph from *Call for the Dead* by John Le Carré; Batsford for an extract from L.T.C. Rolt's *The Thames from Mouth to Source*; the Provost and Scholars of King's College, Cambridge and the Society of Authors as the Literary Representatives of the E.M. Forster Estate for the excerpt from E.M. Forster's *Abinger Harvest*; an extract reproduced by kind permission from *Haslemere* by G.R. Rolston, published in 1978 by Phillimore & Co Ltd; Robson Books for an extract from John Nyren's *The Cricketers of my Time*; Sutton Publishing for a piece from A.P. Bradley & Michael Brown's *Wheels Take Wings*; Froglet Publications for Bob Ogley's *Surrey at War 1939-1945*; David Rose and Graham Collyer for an extract from their *Guildford, The War Years 1939-45*; Chatto & Windus for an extract from *Aristocrats: Caroline, Emily, Louisa and Sarah Lennox 1740-1832* by Stella Tillyard, reprinted by permission of The Random House Group Ltd; Ammonite Books for an extract from *Guildford: A Short History* by Matthew Alexander.

The publishers have endeavoured to contact all holders of copyright, but will be pleased to add any omissions or correct any errors in future editions.

The engravings and line drawings that decorate the start of each chapter are taken from *Wood Engravings of Thomas Bewick* (1753-1828) (Wild Surrey, All People Great and Small, At Work, At Parting); *Excursions in the County of Surrey* (1821) for Guildford Castle (Some Questions of Antiquity) and a view of Dorking (The Towns); *Picturesque Surrey* (1902) by Duncan Moul and Gibson Thompson, for Reigate Castle (Saxons and Normans); *Etchings of Views in the Vicarage of Letherhead* (sic), *Surrey* (1821) by Harriet Dallaway, for 'Elinour Rummin's House' (Good Cheer); *Chertsey and its Neighbours* (1853) by Mrs. S.C. Hall, for the 'Way Bridge' (Landscape and Character), the 'Kitchen in Almner's Barn' (A Home in the Country); *The Brighton Road* (1906) by Charles G. Harper for 'Gatton Hall and "Town Hall"' (On the Hustings); The Collection of the Surrey History Centre for Horsemonger Lane Gaol, Southwark (Crime and Punishment); and William Davison's *New Specimen of Cast-Metal Ornaments and Wood Types* (1780-1858) (Journeys, At Play, At War).

The front cover illustration shows a detail of *Cornfield in Surrey*, (1860) by William Linnell (1826 - 1906), courtesy of The Bridgeman Art Library (Wolverhampton Art Gallery, West Midlands, U.K.).